INDIA AND AMERICA
A STUDY OF THEIR RELATIONS

INDIA *and* AMERICA

A Study of Their Relations

By

PHILLIPS TALBOT *and* S. L. POPLAI

Published for the
COUNCIL ON FOREIGN RELATIONS
by
HARPER AND BROTHERS
New York, 1958

The Council on Foreign Relations is a non-profit insti-
tution devoted to study of the international aspects of
American political, economic and strategic problems. It
takes no stand, expressed or implied, on American policy.
The authors of books published under the auspices of
the Council are responsible for their statements of fact and
expressions of opinion. The Council is responsible only
for determining that they should be presented to the
public.

The Indian Council of World Affairs is a non-govern-
mental, non-profit-making and non-party organization,
founded in 1943 to encourage and facilitate the objective
study of Indian and International Affairs. The Council,
as such, is precluded by its constitution from expressing
an opinion on any aspect of Indian or International
Affairs. Any opinions expressed in this book are, therefore,
the opinions of the authors and not those of the Council.

INDIA AND AMERICA

Copyright, © 1958, by Council on Foreign Relations, Inc.
Printed in the United States of America

All rights reserved, including the right to reproduce
this book or any portion thereof in any form.

For information, address Council on Foreign Relations,
58 East 68th Street, New York 21

SECOND PRINTING

American Book–Stratford Press, Inc., New York

Library of Congress catalog card number: LC 57-8186

10821

ACKNOWLEDGMENTS

WE HAVE made extensive use of the data papers and the comments of the two study groups upon them, which preceded the writing of this joint report. In particular, we have profited from the illuminating discussions by the representatives of the two study groups, who met in June 1956 at Dedham, Massachusetts. We have a particular debt to the chairmen of our respective groups for their help and guidance throughout our work. We also received many valuable suggestions from several individual members of the two study groups, some of whom freely gave us their counsel from the planning of this study to the reading of the final draft of the manuscript. While we are indebted to all the writers of the data papers and members of the study groups, our special thanks are due to Messrs. Walter H. Mallory, Philip E. Mosely and William Diebold, Jr., of the staff of the Council on Foreign Relations, and Messrs. Asoka Mehta, S. Mookerjee and A. Appadorai, members of the Indian Council of World Affairs.

We must also acknowledge our indebtedness to Mrs. Marina S. Finkelstein whose unstinting assistance helped us greatly to overcome the difficulty caused by the two authors working in two continents. Her help in Chapters 7 and 8 in particular was invaluable; without it we would not have finished our work in reasonable time. She has also prepared the index. We thank the Council on Foreign Relations for making her assistance available to us.

In the long and complicated process of carrying out this study we have naturally incurred more debts than we can fully acknowledge. We should like however to thank Miss Lorna Brennan, whose management of administrative affairs contributed much to the success of the Dedham conference, and Robert Valkenier and James Murphy, who kept a record of the proceedings. Like all who engage in research, we are also indebted to librarians: Miss Ruth Savord and her staff at the Council on Foreign Relations, and Mr. Girja Kumar of the Indian Council of World Affairs.

While we received help and advice from many persons and institutions, the two authors alone are responsible for the various statements made in this joint report on Indian-American relations. The two sponsoring Councils bear no responsibility whatsoever for the views expressed in this study.

S.L.P.
P.T.

PREFACE

INDIA and the United States have much in common. Libberty, democracy, national independence, and respect for the individual, are ends to which both countries are dedicated. Each strives for the maintenance of world peace and creation of the kind of world in which every people can pursue these ends in its own way. Sharing many common aims and values, India and the United States also differ in significant ways in their character, experience, and immediate circumstances. In its ten years of independence India has faced, and continues to face, vast problems of political organization, economic development, and the assumption of an independent role in world affairs. During the same decade the United States has found itself more deeply involved in international affairs than ever before in its history. Inevitably, then, there are important divergences in the policies of India and the United States even when they seek similar ends. An inescapable consequence has been criticism in each country of the other's methods and motives.

Some of the differences between these two friendly nations are due to ignorance and misunderstanding, some result from divergent appraisals of the problems they face, and some reflect real, if limited, conflicts of interest. Study, discussion, and the exchange of views, cannot resolve all these differences, but they can help to remove some and clarify the nature of others. It was to help in this important process that the Council on Foreign Relations, of New York, and the Indian Council of World Affairs, of New Delhi—two private, non-profit organizations devoted to the study of international affairs—undertook an examina-

ix

tion of relations between India and the United States. The study was concerned with both agreement and differences, not only in the direct relations of the two countries but also in the relation of each to world problems affecting them both. This book, which grew out of the study, is dedicated to broadening and deepening the understanding by Indians and Americans of these matters: their common interests and differences, the policies of both countries, and the reasons for them.

The proposal for a cooperative study of Indian-American relations had its origin in conversations that took place in 1953 between Dr. A. Appadorai, then Secretary-General of the Indian Council of World Affairs, and Mr. Walter H. Mallory, Executive Director of the Council on Foreign Relations. Early in the next year the two organizations agreed on a plan of work and in the fall of 1954 study groups began their deliberations in New York and New Delhi. The first task of each group was to analyze major aspects of the other country's foreign policy. Papers on an agreed list of topics were exchanged and subjected to criticism and comment by the other group.

This method, which had already been used by the Council on Foreign Relations and the Royal Institute of International Affairs for a study of British-American relations, is arduous but enlightening. The continuing exchange of information, opinion, and criticism sharpens the areas of agreement and disagreement by subjecting the policies of each nation to the critical gaze of the other. Each group requires full and accurate data and a clear presentation of issues to form its judgment. In India the responsibility for preparing this material fell on Dr. Appadorai and his successor, Sundar Lal Poplai. The Council on Foreign Relations entrusted this work to Phillips Talbot, Executive Director of the American Universities Field Staff, who was assisted throughout the study by Marina Salvin Finkelstein. Both groups also drew on papers prepared by outside experts on certain subjects.

To facilitate the exchange of views, Mr. Talbot spent

several weeks in New Delhi during 1955. Then, in June 1956, five members of the Indian group came to the United States for a five-day conference with members of the American group at Endicott House in Dedham, Massachusetts. Mr. Poplai spent the rest of the summer in New York working closely with Mr. Talbot and Mrs. Finkelstein. Later the two authors were able to confer frequently thanks to a year's visit to India and Pakistan that Mr. Talbot made on behalf of the American Universities Field Staff.

The members of the two study groups were:

Indian Council of World Affairs

*A. Appadorai, *Director of the Study Group*
Director, Indian School of International Studies, New Delhi; formerly Secretary-General, Indian Council of World Affairs

G. L. Bansal
Secretary-General, Federation of Indian Chambers of Commerce and Industry, New Delhi

E. P. W. da Costa
Editor, *The Eastern Economist,* New Delhi

D. R. Gadgil
Director, Gokhale Institute of Politics and Economics, Poona

N. V. Gadgil
Vice-Chairman, State Bank of India; formerly Member of Parliament (Congress Party)

B. N. Ganguli
Director, Delhi School of Economics, University of Delhi

*A. D. Gorwala
Administrative Consultant and Journalist; formerly of the Indian Civil Service

K. P. Karunakaran
Lecturer, Indian School of International Studies; formerly Research Associate, Indian Council of World Affairs

* attended conference in Dedham

S. V. Kogekar
  Head of the Department of Political Science, Fergu-
  son College, Poona
*Asoka Mehta
  Formerly Member of Parliament (Praja Socialist
  Party)
V. K. N. Menon
  Director, Indian Institute of Public Administration;
  formerly Professor of Political Science, University of
  Patna
K. M. Panikkar
  Ambassador to France; formerly Member, Indian
  States Reorganization Commission
*S. L. Poplai
  Secretary-General, Indian Council of World Affairs
*V. K. R. V. Rao
  Vice-Chancellor, University of Delhi; formerly Di-
  rector, Delhi School of Economics

Council on Foreign Relations

*Arthur H. Dean, *Co-Chairman*
  Partner, Sullivan and Cromwell; formerly Special
  United States Ambassador to Korea
* Henry M. Wriston, *Co-Chairman*
  President, Council on Foreign Relations; President,
  The American Assembly, Columbia University; for-
  merly President, Brown University
Chester Bowles
  Formerly Ambassador to India
*William Diebold, Jr.
  Director of Economic Studies, Council on Foreign
  Relations
*Marina S. Finkelstein
  Research Assistant, Council on Foreign Relations
*Nevil Ford
  Director and formerly Senior Vice-President, First
  Boston Corporation

*Holden Furber
Associate Professor, History and South Asian Studies,
University of Pennsylvania
*Kenneth R. Iverson
Near East Representative and formerly Director of
Overseas Development Program, Ford Foundation
*Elmore Jackson
Director, United Nations Program, American
Friends Service Committee
*Richard D. Lambert
Assistant Professor, Sociology and South Asian Stud-
ies, University of Pennsylvania
*Walter H. Mallory
Executive Director, Council on Foreign Relations
Clifford B. Marshall
Vice-President and Director, Standard-Vacuum Oil
Company
*Max F. Millikan
Director, Center for International Studies, Massa-
chusetts Institute of Technology
*Philip E. Mosely
Director of Studies, Council on Foreign Relations
*J. Morden Murphy
Vice-President, Bankers Trust Company
*Norman D. Palmer
Professor, Political Science and International Rela-
tions, University of Pennsylvania
*Ithiel de Sola Pool
Director, International Communications Program,
Massachusetts Institute of Technology
*S. Dillon Ripley
Associate Curator, Peabody Museum of Natural His-
tory, Yale University
*Phillips Talbot
Executive Director, American Universities Field
Staff, Inc.

We wish to express our thanks and that of our respective Councils to these men who gave so much of their time, energy, and wisdom to this long and often rather strenuous process. They have contributed much to this study but they have not reviewed the manuscript of this book and bear no responsibility for it or for the views expressed by the authors.

From the beginning it was our hope that the cooperative study would lead to a joint publication. That this hope has been realized is due largely to the ability, hard work, and tact of the two authors and of Mrs. Finkelstein, who worked closely with them during the sixteen months from the end of the Dedham conference to the time the manuscript went to press.

The task assigned to the authors was a most difficult one. They write on their own responsibility, yet as collaborators neither could write exactly the book he would have written alone. They are not spokesmen for the study groups or the two Councils, yet since their book grows out of the cooperative study they have tried to take account of the views expressed in the course of it. They have tried to identify areas of agreement and disagreement in the policies and attitudes of the two countries without either magnifying differences or straining to find consensus where it does not exist. They write for two main audiences: the people of India and of the United States. Therefore they have had to keep constantly in mind the differences between what is common knowledge in each country. Inevitably, some readers in both India and the United States will find some of the information in this book very familiar, but they must bear in mind that there are others to whom the data are new and necessary. Not the least of the hurdles in the way of the two authors was the fact that their manuscript had to pass the review of committees in both Councils. Thus the form and scope of the book have been dictated by its origins and purpose. The authors have justified the confidence placed in them by the two Councils. Overcoming many difficulties of subject and circum-

stance, they have produced a book that throws light on
Indian-American relations and frankly faces the major
issues that join or divide the two countries. The special
significance of the book is that it is a joint product growing out of a cooperative study.

Sundar Lal Poplai, the Indian author, is Secretary-General of the Indian Council of World Affairs, Managing
Editor of *India Quarterly*, and Editor of *Foreign Affairs
Reports* and *Indian Affairs Record*. He has studied at the
Universities of Delhi, London, and Cambridge and has
taught history and political science at the University of
Delhi. He has written and edited numerous articles, books
and pamphlets. Phillips Talbot, the American author, began his study of Indian affairs in 1938. Since then he has
spent some ten years in India as foreign correspondent,
United States naval officer, fellow of the Institute of Current World Affairs, and most recently as Executive Director of the American Universities Field Staff. He has studied at Aligarh University, and has spent considerable time
in the villages of India as well as in its large cities. In addition to writing extensively about Indian affairs, Mr. Talbot has taught courses on South Asia at the University of
Chicago and at Columbia University.

The Indian Council's participation in this work was
made possible by a grant from the Rockefeller Foundation.
The Council on Foreign Relations drew on research funds
provided by the Rockefeller and Ford Foundations and
the Carnegie Corporation.

The Council on Foreign Relations is very grateful to
the American Universities Field Staff for making it possible for Mr. Talbot to devote an important part of his
time to this study.

Although the name of Marina Finkelstein does not appear on the title page of this book, we recognize, as do the
authors, the key role she played in its preparation. Her
many contributions were essential to the success, and indeed the completion, of this study.

Finally we are sure that we speak for all the members of

the study groups when we express the thanks of each to all the others, Indian and American, and to the authors of this book, for the understanding we have all gained in the course of this work. This understanding, of differences as well as of agreement, stands, with this book, as a lasting product of this cooperative endeavor.

A. APPADORAI
ARTHUR H. DEAN
HENRY M. WRISTON

CONTENTS

Acknowledgments   vii

Preface   ix

1. INTRODUCTION   1

2. THE SHAPING OF FOREIGN POLICY   14
   Foreign Affairs in National Life   15
   Shaping Attitudes on Foreign Affairs   20
   Constitutional and Political Practices   26

3. INTERNATIONAL AND DOMESTIC COMMUNISM   35
   Communism as Theory   36
   Policy Development: United States Policy and the
      Soviet Union (1945–1950)   40
   Indian Evaluation of Soviet Goals   52
   The Indian "Bridge" Policy   58
   Military Pacts in Indian-United States Relations   61
   Coexistence and the Hungarian Crisis   64

4. PAKISTAN IN INDIAN-AMERICAN RELATIONS   68
   The Kashmir Problem   71
   American Arms Aid to Pakistan   86

5. EAST AND SOUTHEAST ASIA   95
   The "China Question": to the End of the Civil War   97
   Responses to the Communist Victory   100
   Recognition and Seating in the United Nations   104
   Formosa   107
   Tibet and India's Northeast Frontier Area   111
   Korea   117

Southeast Asia 126
A Look Ahead 135

6. ECONOMIC PROBLEMS IN INDIAN-AMERICAN
   RELATIONS 137

7. COLONIALISM 155
   Past Issues 158
   Contemporary Issues 163
   The Prospects 167

8. HUMAN RIGHTS 169

9. CONCLUSION 184

Index 195

Chapter 1

INTRODUCTION

IN 1945—WHEN World War II ended—India and the United States were virtual strangers to one another. India was still under British rule, its energies concentrated inward on the fight for independence, its foreign contacts limited. The United States was one of the major powers, with global interests, its energies engrossed in the shaping of a world peace in which India was not one of the outstanding problems. Nor had the Indians and Americans had much contact in the past. The American people did, it is true, have some memory of clipper ship trade with India and some knowledge of missionary activities there. Many had followed with sympathy the long Indian struggle against British domination—a struggle which for some had awakened echoes of the earlier American fight for independence. But close contacts between India and the American republic had not been possible nor indeed particularly wanted.

Today neither India nor the United States could ignore each other even if either so desired. Each country wields important influence in world affairs—even though the influence of each differs inherently from that of the other. The major foreign policies of both touch and on occasion clash with each other. And the future role of each nation will affect the core interests of the other. Since 1947, and particularly since 1950, the two peoples have been groping toward a clearer knowledge of each other, toward greater respect, and on occasion toward closer cooperation. Taken

1

in very broad outline this process has been not unsuccessful and in many basic matters relations between the two nations have been friendly. At the same time India and the United States have been divided, on occasion bitterly, in their estimates of each other's intentions and over major problems of policy.

Both in India and the United States many thoughtful persons have been distressed at the misunderstanding and resentment that have followed these differences. Their common hopes for better relations between the two nations are based on the belief that the issues between them have been exaggerated through ignorance on both sides or that they are on the whole neither insoluble nor such that they cannot—many of them—be "lived with" without vital harm to basic national interests. They are convinced also that the two peoples share a common ground of human aspirations, historical development and hopes for the future on which a broader basis for cooperation can be constructed. It is to the joint and positive discussion of present and future foreign policy issues between the two countries that this volume is devoted.

Direct Indian-American relations began in an atmosphere of mutual sympathy. During the war President Roosevelt had lent America's moral support to the Indian struggle for independence. For this Indian leaders were grateful. They wanted to see the growth of friendly relations between a free India and the United States. Even before the transfer of full power to Indian hands and while he was still a member of Lord Wavell's interim government of 1946, Jawaharlal Nehru was eager to establish diplomatic relations. Ambassadors were first exchanged in October 1946. And the United States was the first country outside the Commonwealth that Nehru visited after becoming Prime Minister. The process of becoming acquainted has continued at a brisk pace since then, through vastly increased contacts on many levels.

These increased contacts have not unnaturally disclosed both similarities and differences between the two peoples.

Because quite frequently the differences have tended to obscure the similarities in experience that the two peoples share, it will be valuable to sketch in now the positive factors in the relationship in order to provide a firm background for the subsequent discussion of divisive issues. Thus for example—notwithstanding differences in the circumstances of American and Indian independence movements—both countries have experienced the fervor of nationalism and of democratic ideals. The same sentiments that brought liberty to eighteenth-century America also inspired the leaders of the Indian National Congress throughout their struggle; the American Declaration of Independence made a profound impression on the Indian patriots. Furthermore there is much similarity between the tone of early American and present-day Indian policy. The keen, single-minded and impatient interest of the early generations of Americans in the independence of other colonial areas, particularly in Central and South America, was much like the tone in which Indians now criticize colonialism wherever it exists in Asia and Africa. And the assertive, cocky and suspicious attitude of early American policy-makers—as much an overflow of nationalist fervor and distrust of colonial powers as a reaction to painful memories of earlier European domination—strikes a familiar tone in Indian ears. India is today experiencing similar feelings. Thus Nehru is suspicious, as was George Washington, of "the insidious wiles of foreign influence" and has refused to interweave the destiny and entangle the peace and prosperity of his people "in the toils of European ambition and rivalry."

There are sharp differences, of course, between India's current deep involvement in world affairs and the relative isolation of early America, but the desire for nonalignment in an early period of national growth has had similar roots in both countries. In its first decades the United States was largely taken up with the tasks of building its federal system, of protecting its borders from the incursions of the American Indian tribes and from the encroachments of European colonial ambitions. It was also concerned with freeing its commerce from the interference of European regulations and restrictions and with developing its resources, material and human. In mid-twentieth century, India too has been challenged by the difficult problems of simultaneously consolidating a fiscal, civil and military structure weakened through partition, of integrating the domains of more than five hundred princely states into the Republic, of laying the foundations for a more viable economy and of protecting its borders from outside threats. Along with the desire to avoid international entanglements, both post-Revolutionary America and present-day India have shown no hesitation in lecturing other states on matters outside their own zones of responsibility while they themselves pursued national interests—the westward march for the United States, Kashmir and the French and Portuguese "pockets" in the Indian case—with determination and vigor and with the clear purpose of gaining their full objectives, without compromise.

These parallels in the history of the two countries—which are not vitiated by the sharp contrasts between the circumstances and outlook of eighteenth-century America and modern India—serve to highlight the similarities in the early revolutionary experience of the nations. They also suggest some of the preoccupations that have directed India along much the same route that the United States took in its first decades. By recalling earlier American attitudes they may make it easier for many Americans to recognize some of the emotional force that inspires current Indian policies. On the other hand, a look back at the evolution of American policies since those early days may help Indians to understand that the perspective of time and mood within which current Indian policies have taken shape is itself likely to change over the years and with shifting circumstances.

It is in basic political creeds as well as in the similarity of certain basic goals that the general compatibility of American and Indian long-term interests stands out most clearly. In an age of widespread totalitarianism the governments of both countries seek to hold to the traditions of civil rights and governmental concepts that they inherited to a large degree from the British. Both have in their internal policies rejected the concepts and practices of communism. Liberty and the pursuit of happiness by the individual are the common ideals in India and the United States; both attempt to uphold them against those who would make the individual a tool of state power exercised in the name of an overriding class, community or creed. In both the welfare of the individual is the major goal of state and private action, although the proportions in which such action is blended vary considerably in the two countries.

In their governmental structure both India and the United States are committed to the principle that the state may act only with the consent of the governed and to the practice that this consent shall be expressed through the interaction of contending political parties and through free elections. In both nations civil power dominates the military. The activities of a free press and of an independent judiciary empowered to examine the constitutionality of government action ensure that the constitutional guarantees and fundamental rights have vigilant guardians. In both countries there is a public opinion interested in government action—a public opinion which is not necessarily united in its estimates and criticisms of such action. Although the range of critical opinion is more extensive in the United States, the Indian scene also shows signs of the growth of dissent, even within the Congress party itself. Thus for example in matters involving policy toward Pakistan the government is often criticized for the policies adopted. And in the case of the Hungarian uprising the government found itself urged on to take a somewhat stronger stance than it had in the first few days by the expression of strong criticism within the Congress and the Parliament as well as from the newspapers and private organizations.

Without overdrawing the picture, it is clear that India and the United States share a political heritage and hold in common certain basic assumptions and concepts. These can, in spite of real differences in experience, help cement general Indian-American contacts and on occasion smooth their negotiations on policy.

Even in the very controversial field of economic organization there are parallels which underlie the differences between the two countries. True, in India the state already plays a much more comprehensive role in economic activities than would be acceptable to most Americans except perhaps in a time of national emergency. In India the state does not hesitate to enter into economic activities if it deems such action necessary in the "public interest" or to guide them in detail if it feels such guidance to be required by the needs of India's growth. Furthermore, the leaders of India speak of a "socialistic pattern of society" of a fairly undefined outline in which the state will be committed to take the leading part in economic guidance and activity. At the same time it is important to remember that much private enterprise continues to operate and to expand its activities and that in a number of directions the state has definitely encouraged the growth of the private sector. Furthermore, although of course there are numerous differences, in India as in the United States there is not the severe regimentation of the capitalist, the worker or the consumer that is the hallmark of a totalitarian system. The first concern of both countries is to improve the standard of living of its people and to widen the horizon of opportunities open to them. On the vital principle of making the individual the touchstone of social organization there is no fundamental difference between the two countries. It runs like a thread through all their policies, no matter how unlike they may be in matters of emphasis and detail.

Differences in the Indian and American roles in world affairs arise naturally from the two countries' domestic situations and capacities, from the threats to national interests that they perceive, and from the tasks that are engaging their attention. Perhaps most vital in determining the posture of the two nations in foreign affairs are the differences in national psychology—if this term can be used to describe the complex of each people's memory of its recent experience, the way it applies its cultural values to the solution of current problems, and the manner in which it assesses both the threats confronting the nation and the opportunities open to it. The effect of this complex of memories and attitudes will be apparent throughout this discussion.

The economic potential of each nation also is important in determining the priorities of policy as well as in limiting and shaping the means that are available to implement them. As an advanced industrial nation with one of the highest per capita incomes in the world, with huge developed resources and a highly trained labor force, the United States was not only able to assume the role of the "arsenal of democracy" in two world wars but also to help twice in the reconstruction of the shattered European economies. Its enormous capital resources and its capacity to produce new capital as well enabled it to divert large funds to unlocking the secrets of nuclear energy for man's use in peace or war. The lesson it learned from its attempt between the two wars to remain aloof from international politics and the alarming shape of the postwar world drew the United States after 1945 to assume a new and wider role of participation which it was often able to back up with the necessary resources and strength.

India also has exerted its influence but it is of a different nature and has made itself felt in different ways. India is the most populous non-Communist nation and has an important strategic position. Because of the leadership it has taken in trying to meet the "revolution of rising expectations" through democratic methods and because of the favor—for whatever reasons—which its foreign policy of nonentanglement has found among a number of Asian and African states, India has for some purposes assumed a leading role among Asian states and in world forums as well.

At the same time India is not a fully developed country. It lacks as yet a firm base from which to initiate or sustain without foreign aid a program of economic growth that could adequately meet the increasing expectations of the people and the government. India has a very low per capita income and a slow rate of capital accumulation. About seventy per cent of its people still depend for their livelihood on a system of agriculture that is carried on mainly with obsolete techniques and which is subject to the vagaries of the monsoon. Although the last few years have seen a considerable improvement, the danger that India may not in any given year produce enough food to feed its large and growing population is still a grave one. Thus, although India has many undeveloped as well as unexplored resources and although much progress has already been made, India's economic condition continues to demand the utmost priority in resources, money and national effort. Economic development also requires that India remain at peace and that there be no major international upheaval that might interfere with the orderly execution of such development. To a large extent Indian economic strength and influence, considerable though they are in many matters, still lie mainly in the future, while the influence of the United States is a present thing.

The effect of these differences in economic strength and in national experience is dramatically evident in the major policy patterns of the two nations. It is clear for example in broad security matters. Considering itself directly threatened by the Soviet Union and international communism and being in fact the only state with enough power to offer a decisive measure of opposition to them, the United States has tried to block Communist expansion through diplomacy and other means. In the last few years it has also increased its own military establishment and helped to build up the armed strength of those nations in Europe, Asia and Latin America that shared its concern. In addition the

United States has been willing to use its own resources and men to block the spread of international communism by taking military counteraction, as in Korea. It has also refused to take actions it thought would strengthen international communism, such as, for example, accepting Communist China into the world society under existing conditions. At the same time the United States with its heritage of support for self-determination and with its idealistic, optimistic belief in human progress has coupled its defensive power moves with a new interest in remedying colonial situations and with unprecedented contributions to promoting the economic development of distant countries.

The Indian emphasis has been quite different. Lacking the springs of industrial strength, India has assessed international communism and the kind of threat it poses in Asia in a way that has led to an advocacy of peaceful coexistence with the Communist countries and an emphasis on rapid social and economic development. In Indian eyes, the future role and possible threat posed by the Communist powers are not primarily due to the nature of communism as a political movement. This evaluation, when coupled with the urgent needs of India's domestic programs, has led to a policy of nonalignment, of mediation and conciliation, and of friendship toward both sides. Considerable friction has arisen between the United States and India over this great difference. There have in addition been differences of emphasis between the United States and India on specific policies concerning economic development, "anticolonialism" and human rights, but these have not been of as serious a nature as the differences that have revolved around international communism and in some ways around relations with Pakistan.

Perhaps some of the major differences in approach—as well as some of the similarities—are reflected most clearly in the attitudes of the two countries toward the United Nations. From the beginning it was inevitable that the United States would be a central member of the organization; nothing else was possible, given the American reading of interwar history, American initiative in establishing the United Nations, and the inescapable fact of America's new power. Remembering the disillusioning experience of the League of Nations, the United States has hoped the new international organization would prove able to move effectively against aggression—even if such action came to involve steps against an important state. In order to help circumvent the evident paralysis of the Security Council, the United States has taken the lead in equipping the General Assembly with new instruments for expressing itself on matters involving threats to the peace. In other fields the United States has also supported United Nations efforts to deal with social, economic and political problems, although without any drastic modification of the principle that United Nations action should not intrude upon the limits set by domestic jurisdiction.

While the United States and its allies have been working on the proposition that the road to peace is through strengthening the common security, India is likely to reply: "One does not seek peace through security, but security through peace." This contrast is at the heart of many of the differences in Indian and American positions on questions concerning the United Nations. It explains why India has given such strong and persistent support in that organization to the principle of great power unanimity, in spite of the continuing and glaring absence of such unanimity. India has doubted the wisdom of trying to reform Security Council voting procedure because it has feared the consequences of trying to force through any modifications of the veto more than the consequences of its abuse. It has opposed the creation of any supranational agencies not dependent on great power unanimity because it feared they would exacerbate great power tensions. For the same reason India has maintained the general position that the United Nations should not brand an important and powerful nation an aggressor or conduct military actions against it. Aware of its weakness and its urgent domestic concerns,

India has applied its faith in conciliation and mediation as a general principle to world affairs when they do not directly involve immediate Indian security.

In its United Nations policy India has emphasized the assumptions that peace can be kept only through peaceful means, that under the Charter no member state can be called on to carry out collective security measures against another state without the concurrence of all the permanent members of the Security Council, and that whatever rare enforcement measures might be taken would be strictly of a minor or "policing" nature. Indian participation in the United Nations is based on a concept that soft-pedals its enforcement functions and emphasizes its usefulness as a world forum for negotiation, compromise and discussion, preferably with the active collaboration of a recently awakened Asia. These concepts accord with Indian principles, with the Indian power position and with the Indian concern for enhancing the role of Asian peoples in world affairs. They also increase the contribution which a country like the India of today can make to the work of the United Nations. Similarly, though with different results, the American positions in the United Nations have reflected the numerous and complex responsibilities and interests of the United States.

Other priorities of Indian and American policy—within the United Nations as well as outside—stem from a sense of urgency over social and economic problems that are ever nearer at hand. In spite of a good deal of agitated criticism on both sides, a careful examination of the policy record of both India and the United States shows that in these matters the two countries are divided more by differences of timing and temperament than by basic goals. Thus both Indians and Americans—the Indians perhaps in a more intensely personal way—are deeply conscious of the upsurge that has occurred in Asia and is now spreading across Africa as a result of the impact of the revolutionary Western ideas of national self-determination, government by consent, and of the state as promoter of the welfare of its people. One after another the peoples of the world have come to realize that modern technology can eradicate the starvation and needless disease that have plagued mankind for centuries and that many countries have moved far toward eradicating them. They demand now that they too be freed from the burdens of poverty, illiteracy and economic stagnation. From the Indian perspective the most important task in Asia today lies in devising ways of curing the ills of the people without the use of regimentation and force, in an atmosphere of enthusiasm, self-confidence and democratic self-help.

Although the United States and India are working together in a number of ways toward this difficult end, they are divided in their estimate of the threats that confront free Asia. India puts its emphasis on the dangers of social and economic disintegration which offer the Communists their best opportunities for carrying out indirect aggression and subversion. Therefore India emphasizes the primacy of economic and social measures. At the same time Indian opinion holds not only that military measures fail to meet the situation but also that they exacerbate the real threat by adding to economic and social burdens and that they may heighten the potential military threat because they force the countries against whom they are directed to take countermeasures. The United States agrees to the seriousness of the social and economic dangers but holds that the threat of aggression is also real. It draws the consequence that policies must deal with both threats and that therefore both military alliance and social and economic measures are necessary for the preservation of free Asia.

In spite of adverse criticism in the United States, many Indians feel that their country has accepted the Communist challenge in Asia and that that challenge demands proving to the peoples of the less developed nations that it is possible to move at least as far and as quickly by the methods of democracy as Russia did and China is attempting to do through those of totalitarian communism.

Indians are also conscious—and this recognition is spreading in the United States as well—that their success or failure will have far-reaching consequences for other countries in Asia and Africa facing problems similar to those of India and that its success or failure may eventually win or lose the allegiance of millions of people for the cause of freedom and democracy. Making its own program succeed is India's most urgent problem. Against such a perspective, American criticisms of Indian policy toward Asian countries seem to many Indians to miss the central issue. From the American point of view the same often seems true of Indian policy toward the area. Whether and how the two policies can come to work together toward the accomplishment of a common goal—the growth and development of independent nations in Asia—is one of the central questions to which this volume will address itself.

The governments and people of both India and the United States have a deep, strong, urge to preserve and strengthen their cultural values and democratic institutions and to make possible a better life for themselves and for others. Both nations regard world peace as vital to the achievement of these goals although they differ on the best methods of maintaining it and on the point at which decisive action becomes imperative. Both are conscious that the new weapons which science has placed in man's hands make peace a condition not merely of stability but even of survival. It is on questions of *how* to accomplish their goals that India and the United States have often differed. To understand those differences, it is pertinent to look first at the domestic processes by which foreign policies are shaped in the two countries.

Chapter 2

THE SHAPING OF FOREIGN POLICY

THE FACT that the United States and India are both democracies suggests certain broad similarities in the processes by which they reach major policy decisions. The heart of the matter lies in a common faith in public participation in the decisions of government. The essential concept of freedom of expression and of criticism is fundamental to both political systems. Both try to safeguard the integrity of elections and both allocate basic powers to the legislature. As a result, the executive policy-makers of both countries function under a considerable degree of public and legislative scrutiny. In the absence of strong policy differences such similarities in tradition can play a role in strengthening Indian-American relations. They provide mutually recognizable and acceptable basic assumptions and points of view.

Within the democratic framework, however, the impact of foreign affairs and the ways in which foreign policies are developed in New Delhi and Washington stand in considerable contrast. In India, which is just beginning to raise the vast majority of its people from poverty, illiteracy and apathy, few foreign issues impinge on the interest of the bulk of its citizens and those that do are generally related to fields closely within Indian experience, such as nationalism and anticolonialism. Furthermore, the constitutional and political procedures that have so far been developed in India tend to concentrate influence and authority in a limited group. National attitudes toward

14

foreign relations take shape through the influence of fairly narrow segments of the population.

By contrast, the impact of foreign relations in the United States is spread widely throughout the population. The domestic situation and international position of the United States mean inevitably that most major questions affect more or less directly a great many Americans. A multitude of interested voices speak out on any important issue. The governmental system diffuses the power of decision in foreign as in domestic affairs. Thus we can say that while in India the domestic factors that affect foreign affairs are relatively limited or concentrated, in the United States they are relatively diffused.

Certain features of this phenomenon of concentration in India and of diffusion in America are well known. Prime Minister Nehru's intellectual, emotional and political sway over his country's foreign policy has no parallel in the United States. Nor is there any division of authority in New Delhi to compare with the constitutional separation of powers in the American government. But the matter goes deeper and farther than is often realized, and when misunderstood can inject unnecessary irritants into Indian-American relations.

Foreign Affairs in National Life

Although India's independence is of recent origin, the major roots of its foreign policy reach back into the nineteenth century. Indeed from the founding of the Indian National Congress party in 1885 a number of Indian nationalist leaders had an important interest in establishing the reality of a distinctively Indian outlook on foreign affairs. At its very first meeting the Congress set the tone by passing a resolution protesting against the (British) government of India's impending annexation of Upper Burma. Over the following seventy years the Congress was to adopt more than a hundred resolutions on foreign affairs. Most of them were directed against colonialism, some sought links with anticolonial groups outside of India, all of them underlined the nationalist feeling for the importance of human dignity everywhere.[1]

Immediately after World War II, when the prospect of independence took concrete form, the Congress party reaffirmed its position in the following strong statement concerned specifically with the situation in Burma, Malaya, Indochina and Indonesia but having general significance as well.[2]

To continue imperialist domination over these countries, under whatever name or guise, would be a denial and repudiation of the professions made by the United Nations during wartime and would sow the seeds of future wars. India, desiring the freedom of all Asiatic as well as other countries, would deeply resent the continuation of an imperialist policy in Southeast Asia.

Throughout the struggle for independence the Congress party resolutions on foreign policy had played an important role, but it was played largely within India itself. Understandably enough, many Indians came to feel a satisfaction and a confidence in the identification of their nationalist movement with similar movements elsewhere and with some of the most prominent international issues of the times. Their self-confidence was further buoyed up by the attention which the world's chanceries and press gave the Indian nationalist resolutions as a portent of India's future influence.

The satisfaction and pride with which a substantial part of Indian opinion had come to view the Indian posture in world affairs continued by and large with independence. Indeed there was little reason for it not to, for the foreign policy of independent India continued much in the pattern of Congress party resolutions. Especially in its early

[1] Year after year the Congress passed resolutions of greetings to other peoples under colonial rule: to the people of Egypt, 1924 and 1928; of Palestine, 1928, 1936, 1937, 1938, 1939; of Abyssinia, 1936; of Spain—under fascism—1936; of China—under Japan—1937, 1938, 1939, 1941; of Czechoslovakia, 1938; of Indonesia, 1945; of Indochina, 1945.

[2] All-India Congress Committee, *Background of India's Foreign Policy* (New Delhi, 1952), p. 89.

years, this foreign policy consisted mainly of applying desirable moral standards to situations that did not seem to
most Indians to touch direct Indian political, economic or
strategic interests. With the exception of Kashmir and of
relations with Pakistan in general, the newly freed India
was rarely called upon to assume responsibility for important international problems. In that sense, its foreign policy was generally devoid of concrete action.

Another influence on India's posture in world affairs
has been the fact that by and large the Indian people do
not feel much hereditary or cultural attachment to other
parts of the world. Although the Moslems have a lively
sense of kinship with Islam in general, in cultural terms
the Hindus of India have in the past been oriented inward.
It is true that India did in early times have a cultural and
religious impact on Southeast Asia but on balance modern
India has been a receiver of foreign—particularly Moslem
and British—influences. Furthermore there are few if any
groups in India that depend in any personal sense on
foreign developments.

Until recently, then, Indian foreign policy has consisted
mainly of the expression of values that are important to
the Indian people and has not been much subject to the
demands of concrete, multiple and conflicting Indian
interests. At the same time, the policy positions that independent India took attracted attention abroad and gave
India an international prestige—again excepting Kashmir
and Pakistan—and this at a time when at home there was
little to encourage national pride. Famines, the wounds of
partition, the difficulties of establishing a new administration and of settling on the outlines of domestic development—all these as well as a host of other problems made
the going hard. At such a time it was even more satisfying
than it might otherwise have been to see India exercising
influence on the Dutch "police actions," to observe the attention with which India was heard in the United Nations,
to see its role in Korea and in Indochina, and to note the
increasing number of foreign dignitaries who felt it worth

while to call on Prime Minister Nehru. Furthermore, many Indians continued to derive satisfaction from the vigor with which two of the main lines of their government's foreign policy—anticolonialism and opposition to military pacts—made their old imperialist opponents conscious of the growing political influence of Asian states.

Also important was the fact that this world-wide prestige came to India without either the need for special financial outlays abroad—except in some aid in Nepal and Burma—or for strengthening its military establishment. Almost any country would enjoy such a situation of influence achieved without much cost, but for India it was and is an especially rare and fortunate position because a foreign policy involving more than minimal outlay, however successful, could have been pursued only at the expense of vital priorities in internal development plans. It is not surprising therefore that for this reason as well as for others only a few small groups of little strength have persistently opposed the government's foreign policy. With these small exceptions, this policy has so far received the overwhelming acclaim of Indian opinion.

The United States with its much longer history as an independent nation functions in a far more variegated complex of international contacts. Foreign affairs have had personal meaning to American commercial interests since the days of the clipper ships, to American church members who have sent missionaries abroad for at least as long, to the immigrants and their descendants, who have retained personal ties with "the old country," to manufacturing and investment concerns in modern times, and recently to the nation as a whole which has sent soldiers and very substantial aid abroad. Since the passing of the age when European coalitions and conflicts dominated international politics—an age in which the United States was nevertheless twice involved in world war—America has been intent on adjusting its policies to a new and unforeseen world in which it has, whether it liked it or not, become one of the centers of power. The quick breakdown after World War

II of the hoped-for coalition of victors, the predicament of an exhausted Europe, the crises in the Near and Far East, the portentous implications of the development of atomic weapons—all these as well as other stresses and strains have thrown responsibilities on the United States far beyond any previous experience.

Its response has been to adopt new postures and to undertake new commitments. These have taken the unprecedented form of a system of alliances and an equally unprecedented outpouring within a decade of some sixty billion dollars in foreign economic and military aid. There have been major successes—the vigorous recovery of Western Europe and the blunting in some areas of overtly aggressive drives by the Soviet Union—and failures such as the China policy. But none of the courses of action proposed in the great public and Congressional debates could guarantee the peace and security most Americans had expected to be the fruits of victory in World War II; moreover, all contained incalculable risks. Although the postwar period has brought a sense of increased world prestige, it has also brought to most Americans a sense of anxiety, of heavy responsibilities and of a complexity of involvements previously unknown. Foreign policy has thus become an issue of moment to every taxpayer, who must ultimately bear the heavy costs involved, and to every citizen, who over a period of years has had to become accustomed to living in the shadow of serious threats to the national security.

There is therefore a major difference in the degree of involvement in foreign affairs that the Indian and American peoples have so far experienced. This difference makes for a sharper focusing of public attention on a smaller number of foreign policy issues in India than is possible in the United States. An irritant in Indian-American relations is one result. When outsiders castigate India's policies as "neutralist"—as some Americans often do—Indians assume that they are calling into question one of the great areas of faith and confidence that new India has achieved.

Conversely, when Indians attack American policies there are many Americans who regard them as too little aware of the complexities of world problems for which they have much less responsibility.

Recently, however, what might be called a mellowing of some lines of Indian foreign policy has become evident. As the government of India and its Prime Minister have become more directly involved in practical issues, the awareness of the need for compromise has increasingly entered into Indian foreign policy. On the American side, too, there has been more evidence of late that the problems of assuring their national security have not blinded Americans to other considerations that Indians regard as important.

Although the role of foreign affairs in Indian public life has not been all-embracing or as crucial as it is in the United States, there is every likelihood that the disparity will decrease with India's growing involvement in issues that touch its economy and security.

Shaping Attitudes on Foreign Affairs

It is far simpler to describe the influences at work on the shaping of foreign policy attitudes in India than in the United States. In India the shaping of these attitudes has for three decades been very largely personified by Jawaharlal Nehru. His influence was felt from the moment he assumed an active role in the nationalist movement. It was he who breathed life into the foreign affairs activities of the Congress party, who directed its foreign affairs research and who in 1936 led the All-India Congress Committee to create a foreign department to seek direct cooperation with organizations abroad in the fight for Indian freedom. Quite frequently it was he who drafted and moved the party's resolutions on foreign issues. In the 1930's he could be found for example addressing crowds of tens of thousands of middle class and peasant listeners on the meaning of the Spanish civil war or Italy's conquest

of Ethiopia. Between prison terms he ranged across Europe
and Asia as a spokesman for the Indian nationalist movement, starting in the process to accumulate a store of information that is today equaled by few foreign ministers.
His exhortations were not in every case accepted by his
compatriots, as when in 1942 he deferred to Gandhi's desire not to organize the people against the threatened Japanese invasion of India. But this was exceptional. After the
war, it was again Nehru who gave the lead to the Congress
party, to most of the press, to nationalists in the universities and to others through his interpretation of the evolv-
ing international situation. It was he who inspired the
calling of the significant Asian Relations Conference in
1947. More than anyone else, he readied India for the international role it assumed when independence came.

Since independence, Prime Minister Nehru's charismatic leadership has, if anything, been even more pervasive in the shaping of foreign affairs attitudes. He has
continued to draft and propound foreign policy resolutions for the Congress party and to guide public attitudes
through constant speaking and frequent writing. In addition, as Prime Minister, Minister of External Affairs and
leader of the House of the People, he has personally formulated the government's policy with his usual vigor and
guided the Parliament in its implementation.

It would be naïve, of course, to ascribe to one individual
all the forces that shape a nation's outlook on the world.
Nehru's role is both more subtle and less solitary than a
bare outline might suggest. It is more subtle because his
formulations reflect not only his own thinking but a sensitive appreciation of the concepts of national interest that
are widely accepted by articulate Indian opinion. Thus it
is possible to say that the Nehru government's foreign policies in their broad outline have been solidly rooted in full
support by the two houses of Parliament and in overwhelming public approval and that whatever dissent may
exist is aimed mainly not at the broad principles but at
their specific applications. Moreover, Nehru's role is less

solitary than is frequently imagined because foreign policy is formulated in the midst of various domestic influences and pressure groups, the presentation of the views of other governments, and the staff work of the Indian diplomatic services and Ministry of External Affairs.

There have, it is true, been instances of opposition on foreign policy matters, not only within the country but even within the Congress party. The difference between Gandhi and Nehru on proper policy toward Japan during the war has already been mentioned, while early in World War II the late Subhas Chandra Bose declared for closer association with both Japan and Germany. In 1950 Purshottam Das Tandon favored a "harder" policy toward Pakistan than did Nehru. Both Bose and Tandon resigned from the presidency of the Congress party before their terms expired, and no third proponent of a differing foreign policy has since been elected to the chair. Some differences have continued to be heard—particularly on Pakistan and also on Goa and the Hungarian uprising of 1956. But so far the opposition within the governing party that has been expressed in foreign policy matters has been mainly of a sort that could either be won over by talking out matters or successfully overcome or that has had little practical significance.

Outside the Congress there are some political groups that openly criticize Nehru's foreign policy but they lack power to implement their dissent. Thus the Socialists— divided among themselves as they are—agree in criticizing Nehru for what they consider to be his "softness" toward communism and Communist powers; the Jana Sangh criticizes his "softness" toward Pakistan, the ultranationalists his "softness" toward Portugal, and the Communists his "softness" toward the "imperialist Western powers." All these critics are weak and divided. The Communist Party of India has gone through sharp internal upheavals in groping toward the correct "line." And its course has not been made easier by the cold treatment it received from Bulganin and Khrushchev during their visit in 1955 and by the necessity for supporting Prime Minister Nehru's foreign policy that was one of the fruits of that visit.

Aside from the political parties, the press exercises perhaps the broadest influence on foreign policy attitudes. The best of India's newspapers devote considerable space to foreign affairs and to discussion of foreign affairs on a fairly high level. They are not backward in expressing dissent from or criticism of particular measures, especially where Indian representatives appear to be feeling their way and the prestige of India is directly involved. For example, there was the liveliest discussion in the newspapers during the winter of 1952 over Krishna Menon's efforts to arrange a Korean truce, and again in 1956 over his actions in the United Nations during the Hungarian crisis. However, only a very few journals of small circulation are aggressively critical of Nehru's foreign policy. Most newspapers of large circulation give general support; nor would it be easy for them to be highly critical in view of the widespread satisfaction with the foreign policy of the Indian government. Thus, radically critical discussion of that policy is rarely found.

This brief synopsis points out the overriding present influence of Nehru on Indian attitudes toward foreign relations: his is the guiding hand that shapes the policy and there are few to criticize his decisions. The thoughtful observer may well wonder whether confusion will necessarily reign after Nehru passes from the active governmental scene. Difficult as such a question must be to answer, it would nevertheless seem that under broadly similar conditions a successor from the Congress party would be likely to follow a generally similar foreign policy. The lines of national interest have slowly clarified in the public mind. No drastic changes should be expected from possible successors although differences of emphasis, imagination and drive are likely. Changes may be expected to come rather as conditions change in the world and within India and as they bring with them a wider diffusion of influences impinging on foreign policy.

Diffusion of influences is the hallmark of American foreign policy formulation, both within the governmental structure itself and outside it. In the United States as in other free countries much of the general public, a conglomerate of many groupings, takes little part in foreign affairs but responds to major stimuli. More important in day-by-day influence and continuing interest is what Gabriel Almond has called the informed and interested "attentive public," the government executives, legislators and civil servants; the editors, analysts, and propounders; and the advocates of special group interests.[3] Tocqueville's perceptive comment on Americans' disposition to further aims they consider desirable by forming private organizations retains much truth. Ethnic groups —often with their foreign-language press—business and labor organizations, agricultural organizations and veterans' groups, women's organizations, religious bodies and other groups formulate attitudes of their own on both domestic and foreign affairs. In striking contrast to India, which has no more than a dozen nonofficial institutions interested in foreign affairs, there are in the United States nearly 5,000 private organizations concerned in one way or other with world affairs. Some sixty of them—having a combined but overlapping membership of about 125,000,-000 persons—belong, for example, to the Conference Group of United States National Organizations on the United Nations. All of these groups on many occasions express their views directly to the President, the State Department, committees of Congress and individual Congressmen.

Furthermore, many other channels are open to strongly organized groups. They speak and write and exert influence through their own organizations, through public forums, and through the mass media of newspapers, magazines, and—if they have enough money—radio and television. While very few, if any, of these media are devoted mainly to foreign affairs, through their joint impact most

[3] See *The American People and Foreign Policy* (New York: Harcourt, Brace, 1950), especially Chapter 7.

citizens are exposed to a wide range of appeals and commentaries on major foreign affairs.

Does the multiplicity of influences that touches many Americans—both in public and private life—make for chaos in foreign policy? Does it make foreign policy more subject to shifting moods than to rational analysis of problems, to domestic political demands, to personal ambitions, to persons from the "extreme fringes?" Some Americans and many foreign commentators believe that it does. For example, the widely publicized onslaught of the late Senator McCarthy on the State Department and the Voice of America was well noted abroad and has had an impact there thought by many to be out of proportion to its actual influence. Nevertheless, there is an impression in India that there is or has been a hysterical fear of communism and communists in the United States and that this fear has resulted in what are considered rigidities and immature policies in American foreign relations. Americans on the other hand are less inclined to be disturbed over the lasting effect of the McCarthy campaign because of their belief that the wide-open forum must afford a platform for the extremes of opinion as well as for the effective center. There is conviction furthermore that the operation of many diverse influences on American opinion has in fact helped the country to define and to serve the national interest and to meet the crises of modern times both in war and in peace.

What has been said above suggests that the term "public opinion" means one thing when applied to India and another when applied to the United States. Many Americans, accustomed to diversity of opinion, tend to regard Indian public opinion on foreign affairs more as a cheering-section for Nehru than as an independent, critical force. Many Indians, by contrast, look upon the evolution of American public opinion as a rough-and-tumble process in which the sensibilities of many people, including those of other countries, can be bruised and in which one strong influence can cancel out another more by skill and volume in communication than by weight of argument. Here, again, as in the question of the role of foreign policy in national life, the disparity will probably diminish as Indian interests become more directly involved, as education spreads in India and as more groups identify foreign policy causes with their personal welfare. Particularly, the disparity would be likely to decrease if a less charismatic leader should succeed to Nehru's responsibilities.

Constitutional and Political Practices

Having before independence had extensive experience with British-style parliamentary institutions, the Congress party never seriously questioned the adoption of that form of government for a free India. Thus in the Indian central government the familiar pattern has been repeated: a Parliament that is the supreme organ of government; an Executive that is part of Parliament but tends to dominate it; a Prime Minister who is provided by the majority party and who picks his Council of Ministers from among members of Parliament, if necessary putting a desired Cabinet Minister up for election to Parliament. The Prime Minister and his colleagues, operating on the principle of joint responsibility, control as in Britain the business of the two Houses of Parliament. In the lower House, particularly, they set the days of debate, control the initiation of money bills and exercise a strict discipline over the party members. The Cabinet makes diplomatic appointments without obtaining the approval of the House. The role of the House in the treaty process is minor. If information is desired from the Executive, a member of Parliament may address questions to the appropriate Minister. In this process the Minister of External Affairs may be criticized, but in the absence, to date, of an opposition party likely to provide an alternative government, the Minister (Nehru) is not subjected, as he would be in Britain, to the continuing scrutiny of a member of Parliament who may hope one day to succeed him and who is subject to the discipline of an opposition party.

It is true that Parliament has control over the Prime Minister in the sense that it can vote a motion of adjournment or censure, deny funds and reject government bills and policies. Under present circumstances, the substantial Congress party majority, its strong party discipline, and the respect in which Prime Minister Nehru is held, render the possibility of such motions being passed largely academic. In the absence of a meaningful opposition party that could hope to govern in the near future and that would in turn be the result of a changed political climate within India, the continuing control of the House of the People by the Executive is inevitable.

This does not mean that ordinary members of Parliament have no opportunity whatever to influence the Prime Minister's policy. As issues arise they are first discussed within the parliamentary Congress party, and in this forum party members are free to express their views fully, although it follows from what has already been said that this opportunity is seized more often in domestic than in foreign matters. As a result of suggestions at the Congress party meeting the Prime Minister may on occasion modify his position. But once the issue reaches the floor of the House each member is expected to obey the party whip. Furthermore each member's unwavering support is virtually assured by the highly centralized Indian parliamentary nominating and election procedure. Thus an Indian politician—unless he happens to be one of the few independents—can be elected to Parliament only if he has served his party well enough to receive from its parliamentary board a so-called "ticket" to stand in a constituency as the Congress party's candidate. The individual politician's position vis-à-vis his party is further weakened by the fact that he has practically no political plums under his control. Furthermore, if he should have strong differences with his party and wish to press them, it would be incumbent upon him to resign from it—a critical step which few politicians would care to hazard, especially on foreign policy matters. All these considerations assure that members of Parliament regularly follow the party whip.

American political structure and practice stand in striking contrast to the Indian pattern. The separation of powers between the Executive and the Congress and between the federal and state governments, which was designed by the founding fathers to prevent an undue concentration of power in any one hand, has resulted in a diffusion of responsibility and in a premium on cooperation between the various units. Within the federal system the President and Congress possess, as it were, segments of various powers; to exercise the functions of government they must work together or else they can paralyze each other.

In terms of foreign affairs the President has substantial powers with which to meet the responsibility for foreign policy which, according to the constitution, is primarily his. He alone commands the full information resources of the government. He alone negotiates with foreign powers and he can on his own enter into executive agreements and joint declarations with other governments. As Commander in Chief he can also take decisions that vitally affect foreign policy issues. In contrast to the situation in India, the Cabinet is considered the President's agent and is responsible to him alone. Although the Senate must give approval to the original appointment, Cabinet members are not subject to Congressional discipline nor can they serve in the Congress while in the Cabinet. In recent years foreign policy problems have come to involve practically all government departments as well as special organs such as the Central Intelligence Agency and also the National Security Council which was set up specifically for the purpose of coordinating major policy proposals and decisions.

Although the powers of the President are far less sweeping than those of the Indian Prime Minister, it is generally recognized that they are adequate for decisive action in critical situations. For example, these powers were sufficient to effect the transfer of fifty American destroyers to Britain in exchange for military base rights in 1940, and to commit the United States to continue the war against Nazi Germany jointly with the other United Nations on condition that none of the allies make a separate peace. Or to take a more recent example, the first American reactions to the North Korean aggression were registered by the President on his own authority. These powers have been under challenge—through substantial support for the proposed Bricker constitutional amendment that would seek to curb the Executive's scope in international agreement—but they remain undiminished.

Nevertheless, the President cannot for any length of time function independently of Congress, for there are few if any legislatures in the world with comparable power in the determination of a nation's foreign policy. Although even a Congress of the same party as the President tends to safeguard its power jealously, the difficulties of operation that are built into the system are usually augmented when one or both Houses of Congress come under the control of another political party—as has been the case since the 1954 national election.

There are many points at which cooperation between President and Congress is essential if a consistent long-term foreign policy is to be developed. Only a few need to be mentioned here. The Senate—which in the American system has more power in foreign affairs than the lower House—has the power to pass on or disapprove diplomatic nominations made by the Executive, and it must give its advice and consent to the ratification of treaties by a two-thirds vote. Nor can a program proposed by the President become law without approval of the two Houses. Their participation goes beyond simple approval or disapproval of the Executive's proposals. Both have committees dealing with foreign affairs which have authority to discuss, amend, bottle up or report favorably or unfavorably on any measure the President proposes. An unfavorable report will usually mean the defeat of the measure or serious amendment. Generally speaking, foreign policy measures are sent first to the Senate, where membership on the Committee on Foreign Relations is particularly sought after. In such circumstances it is small wonder that the cooperation of the Chairman of the Senate Committee on Foreign Relations is a valuable asset to the Executive. Furthermore, the Senate as a whole can also initiate foreign policy recommendations through resolutions sent to the President. In view of the active part played by the Senate and its powers in foreign policy, the habit of including Senators, and also Representatives, on international delegations and preparatory commissions dealing with international affairs has been on the increase.

The greatest influence of the House of Representatives on foreign policy probably derives from the power of the purse, as it alone can initiate an appropriation bill. Like the Senate, the House does not have to accept an Executive proposal but can reject it or emasculate it or even present new proposals of its own. With foreign policy requiring ever-increasing sums of money in recent years, the importance of the House has grown. On occasion it has even seemed to many that it has trespassed on the functions of the Executive through the device of "riders" attached to appropriation acts, as in the 1956 attempt to limit aid to Marshal Tito after his *rapprochement* with Moscow. The process of Executive persuasion must therefore extend to the House as well as to the Senate if the President's program is to be fulfilled. That such persuasion can often work successfully was demonstrated during the consideration of the same appropriation bill; a move by some Congressmen to bar the President from providing further aid to India—a move strongly opposed by the President— was finally voted down.

A device not generally practiced in India but which has attracted much attention there is the investigation process by which committees of Congress obtain information on matters within their jurisdiction and seek—particularly in foreign affairs—to close the gap in information between the Executive and themselves. The committees may request Executive departments to provide information in written form, they may hear witnesses testifying on behalf of these departments, or they may conduct their own investigations of the procedures and policies of the Executive. In spite of some abuses and occasional political misuse, the investigative function of the Congress is a legitimate and traditional one and is frequently conducted on a high and expert level. As people abroad tend to hear mainly about those investigations that relate to foreign affairs, it should be pointed out that the Congressional investigation is used even more freq iently for domestic issues and that it can be just as rough and ready in those issues as it is sometimes in matters of foreign policy.

Another sharp difference between Indian and American practices is found in the role of the individual legislator. In strong contrast to the Indian procedure, national parties and elections in the United States tend to be controlled on a state rather than on a national basis. Although there are strong reasons which impel the state units toward cooperation with the national organization of their party, they control their own sources of strength and are not as easy to discipline from the center as they are in India. Under extreme pressure state party units may even leave their national party, although an event like the "bolt" of the Texas Democrats to Eisenhower in 1952 is rare.

The federal legislator is elected for a fixed term which is different from that of the President. He is selected to stand for election by a state or local party convention or an intraparty election known as the party primary. It is therefore the members of the party within the local or state organization who decide whom they wish to put up for election. In contrast to the Indian procedure, the selection of the legislative candidate is not likely to be made by a national "high command" in Washington but rather on a state or local basis. This party candidate then campaigns in the election. Thus it may come to pass that a politician who stands well with his constituency may be, and not infrequently is, sent to Congress without the support or even against the opposition of the President and the national party organization.

Aside from differences in actual constitutional practice, another characteristic of the American system that has seemed puzzling to many Indians arises from the openness of the American political process. This openness makes possible the public airing of differences among the President's advisors and within Congress to a degree that has on occasion deeply shocked Indian sensibilities. Thus for example during the debate over the proposed American wheat loan to India in 1951, which set the pattern for further economic and technical aid to India, a full public hearing was given to Congressional and private views that there was no political justification for giving aid to India and that no allotment of food grains, no matter how large, would make a lasting contribution to the solution of the problem presented by an unfavorable balance of population to resources. The duration of the debate and the criticism and invective expressed in it scarred Indian susceptibilities and to that extent were a setback to good Indian-American relations. Yet, in the long view, this uninhibited discussion resulted in the achievement of an American consensus that could not have been brought about by Executive edict alone.

Similarly in 1956, Indian opinion, which is especially sensitive to what it considers any misreading of its nonalignment policy, was confused and annoyed over the sequence of contrasting and apparently inconsistent statements about American attitudes toward neutralism made by President Eisenhower, Vice President Nixon, and Secretary of State Dulles. It should be kept clearly in mind however that these statements, as well as the criticisms they stirred up in America, constituted steps in a continuing groping toward a consensus on a difficult issue that had not previously been faced squarely. Nor should Indians allow their sensitive reactions to obscure the fact that the Indian Parliament, Indian leaders, the Indian press and Indian public opinion have on occasion also thrown very rough brickbats at the United States.

Within India there crops up an occasional feeling that the American constitutional machinery, however valuable it was in balancing the powers and ambitions of men in the times of the founding fathers, has lately lacked adaptability to the new conditions in which the United States finds itself. On balance, however, it can be argued that the American constitutional system has in fact proved adequate and flexible enough to carry through, since World War II, the most profound readjustment of the nation's foreign policies in its history—such as the Truman Doctrine, the Marshall Plan, Point Four and NATO. Many Americans believe that despite disruptive activities by some Senators and others, despite divisions over foreign relations within both the Republican and the Democratic parties, despite the publicized conflicts of testimony by officers of the administration, American responsibilities in this field have been discharged in a sober and adequate way.

How important to Indian-American relations are these differences in their domestic political situations? Some of the differences are more conspicuous than fundamental. For example, it is primarily faulty understanding that evokes impatience and annoyance with the contrasting constitutional and political processes. As these become more familiar they need cause no more difficulty in Indian-American relations than do similar contrasts in the case of Anglo-American relations. Similarly, no serious trouble should arise from the contrasts between the kinds of influences that bear on the formulation of foreign relations attitudes in the two countries. If Americans are surprised at a seeming lack of public criticism of foreign policy in India, they sometimes discount too much the strength of Indian public feeling. On the other hand if Indians are confused by the seeming babble of voices in America on major issues, they may overlook the underlying consensus and continuity of purpose in the United States. Greater familiarity and better understanding can alleviate these misapprehensions.

Other difficulties arise from the fact that America's contacts with the world are more numerous and more varied than India's. The Indian response to foreign policy issues often seems simpler and more clear-cut than the American because Indians do not need to resolve the same complex equations of conflicting forces and interests that confront the United States. The occasional impatience with which many Indians view the compromises that America feels it necessary to make and with which many Americans regard the seeming failure of India to face the full complexity of international problems may be understandable, but it is none the less real. However, as Indian experience expands, the situation seems to be easing. In 1948, the firmness of America and its allies in defeating the Soviet blockade of West Berlin by peaceful means did not make much impression on an India whose interests did not then comprise European developments. On the other hand, in 1956, the fighting in Hungary and in Egypt touched Indian sensibilities deeply with the result that American policy in these situations had a strong—and favorable—impact on Indian opinion.

Despite misunderstandings and annoyances, their common reliance on democratic processes creates a strong bond of sympathy between India and the United States. Democracy arouses expectations of certain patterns of national behavior. There is a strong predisposition in favor of respect for human rights. Because policies are evolved through discussion and multi-staged decision, there is a promise that they will not be arbitrary. There is a deep aversion to war. The sharing of these basic values provides a framework of common understanding that should be kept in mind as we turn to examine the issues on which Indian and American policies differ.

Chapter 3

INTERNATIONAL AND DOMESTIC
COMMUNISM

THERE IS, as we have seen, much in the Indian and American tradition and practice that draws these democracies together. There is also much in their broad foreign policy goals that is close to people in both countries. And yet these similarities, these common bonds, may be as misleading as they are enlightening. This is so because they make it easier to underestimate the extent to which the specific courses of each country have been based on widely differing perspectives of the political topography of the world.

That this is so is hardly surprising nor is it a condition confined to Indian-American relations alone. Historical national experience, contemporary pressures and needs, current priorities and resources, geographical position, psychological and emotional outlook—all these combine to form a focus peculiar to each nation in the world. Thus, to India, relations with Pakistan are of the utmost urgency while to the United States they are not. In the Indian view, military pacts only add to the evils which they are supposed to correct; to the United States they are an essential part of defense. In Indian eyes Communist China —the close and dynamic neighbor—ought for a variety of reasons to be drawn onto the international scene, while to the United States it remains an aggressor and a continuing menace. And there are other differences of acute importance.

35

Underlying these points of conflict, and indeed intruding into almost all areas of policy, is another difference of opinion. This concerns the divergence between India and America on the twin topics of the nature of communism and of Soviet intentions.[1] So acute have these differences been on occasion that they have tended to obscure the broad community of interest between India and the United States and have interfered with the calm discussion of topics which in themselves have or should have little connection with matters concerning either communism or the Soviet Union.

Although attitudes toward communism and the Soviet Union are inextricably linked to each other, they can nevertheless be differentiated to a certain degree. We start therefore with a look at Indian and American views on the political tenets and practices of communism and on its economic and social programs. Then we shall consider the implications for Indian-American relations of Soviet power in Europe and Asia along with the Western nations' countermeasures and the problems of coexistence.

Communism as Theory

It would be wrong to try to compare "the" Indian view of communism with "the" American view. In both countries there is a variety of judgments on communism and even more on how to deal with it. But some generalizations are possible. First of all, so far as domestic communism is concerned, hostile reactions have been widespread in both countries. Both nations have been strongly influenced by traditions of individual freedom and of responsible and responsive government; both find the doctrines of class war, dictatorship of the proletariat, liquidation of all opposition and suppression of individual liberties generally repugnant. Both realize that their domestic Communist parties dance to tunes called by Moscow or perhaps increasingly by Peking. Furthermore, both have had

[1] Chinese communism is discussed in Chapter 5.

unfortunate experiences with their domestic Communists. Indian leaders remember, for example, the collaboration of the Indian Communists with the British government during the second war, their armed insurrection in 1948 in the Telengana region of Hyderabad, and their continuing attempts to exploit the conflicts of linguistic and other divisive groups within India. The government has therefore taken strong measures against Indian Communists. Under the wide powers given the Executive by the Preventive Detention Act passed in accordance with Article 22 of the Constitution, the government imprisoned thousands of Communists for disruptive activities. Furthermore Prime Minister Nehru and the ruling Congress party have repeatedly charged the Communist party with being anti-national tools of foreign influence and purveyors of inadequate and outdated dogmas. The installation after the 1957 elections of a Communist party ministry in Kerala State, pledged to administer the State within the framework of the Indian constitution, may perhaps require the Congress party to redraw its plans to meet this new Communist challenge at home.

In the United States, experience has bred profound distrust of the American Communist party. The postwar revelations of the long reach of Soviet espionage, its penetration into government posts and atomic energy secrets, all these both served to revive prewar suspicions of communism and caused widespread alarm over domestic Communist activities. This alarm led to a series of Congressional and state investigations; to the initiation and tightening of various "loyalty programs;" to the enactment of the Internal Security Act of 1950; and to Congressional action in 1954 purporting to outlaw the Communist party, depriving Communist-infiltrated trade unions of certain legal privileges, allowing Congress in some cases involving national security to deprive witnesses of the immunity of the Fifth Amendment, and establishing the death penalty for peacetime spying.

In spite of this record of vigorous anti-Communist action in both countries, it is curious to note how distorted a picture each has formed of the other in this regard. To most Americans it has been the international attitude of India toward communism that has been apparent, while its stern domestic policy remained largely unknown. And as far as most informed Indians are concerned, it was the "McCarthyite excesses" of loyalty investigations that all too often seemed to be the sum total of American anti-Communist activities. Thus groups in each country have castigated the policy of the other on the basis of insufficient knowledge. As more Americans become aware of the Indian attitude and as the phenomenon of "McCarthyism" recedes into the background, it can be expected that a more sober and respectful attitude may develop in each country concerning the policy of the other toward its domestic Communist problems. In this way at least one element of irritation in Indian-American problems may be removed.

More pervasive differences between the two countries are revealed in the interpretations favored in each of communism as an international movement. Here again it is unsafe to generalize as there are many crosscurrents of opinion, but broadly speaking the Indian intellectual has been the more stirred by and hospitable to the social and economic theories propounded by Marx and some of his followers. For one thing, to a generation of Indian intellectuals maturing restively under British rule the Marxian criticisms of feudal and capitalist-dominated societies often seemed to apply to India. Even more, Lenin's theories of war and imperialism as "historical" explanations as well as his moral condemnation of colonialism seemed to give answers to the dilemmas that confronted the Indian anti-colonialist. The attractions of the goals of the classless society and the withering away of the state, together with a professed passion for peace, also played a share in establishing a favorable frame of mind.

After the Bolsheviks came to power they and then the Soviet leaders built on this favorable foundation by an unceasing anticolonial propaganda in Asia and by a cordial attitude toward anticolonial activities and organizations. In the 1920's Nehru and other Indians who visited the Soviet Union were impressed with the rapid industrial growth of Russia, the spread of education and literacy and health and with what was described in the Soviet Union as a scientific approach to economic development. Many leaders of the colonial peoples thus became accustomed to think of communism as offering definite answers to their problems and of the Soviet leaders as sympathetic to them and hostile to their imperial masters.

Against these views is the strong suspicion and skepticism of communism—"pure" or otherwise—that is prevalent in the United States. This is founded on several convictions: that communism misreads the historical processes that have fundamentally transformed the conditions against which Marx protested; that the Communist theories of war and imperialism similarly misread the process which has led to the withering away of colonialism, and indeed were expounded cynically to advance the group and national interests of Communist leaders; that far from promoting any withering away of the state or any protection to the citizen against official arbitrariness, a national Communist government must by internal compulsions be totalitarian. Furthermore, to most Westerners the portrait of the Soviet Union as a disinterested anticolonial power seems highly simplified—ignoring as it does for example the zigzags of Soviet policy toward China in the 1920's and of Soviet policy toward Europe in the 1930's, as well as in later years.

These differences have their repercussions and influence in the economic field as well. Although Prime Minister Nehru has repeatedly and firmly stated that the Indian choice has been made—and made decisively—in favor of democratic government, there is much in Communist economic theory and experience as exemplified in the Soviet Union that has seemed attractive to Indian thinkers to a degree that would be extremely rare in the United

States. Reserving a discussion of state participation in the economic process for a later chapter, we need recall here only that to many Indians the Soviet Union's experience in forcing through quick industrialization has seemed to have much more in common with the needs and demands of India than what they regard as the more leisurely development of the United States and Britain. Most American opinion on the other hand, in addition to doubting the superior effectiveness of a totalitarian economy, regards it as discredited by its terrible human and social costs.

Americans look on communism as a moral abomination and treat it with clear-cut and impatient indignation. Indian attitudes can be described as more mixed. Except for Socialist and some right-wing groups, Indian opinion does not pose the issue in moral terms and is therefore more tolerant in its appraisal of Communist theory and in its dealings with the Soviet Union. The revelations concerning Stalin's rule made by Nikita Khrushchev at the Twentieth Communist Party Congress held at Moscow in February 1956, and the Hungarian uprisings, have so far not had any significant concrete policy effects. Shocking they were, but they seem to have confirmed the Indian government in its conviction that the "liberalization" process within the Soviet Union and the East European countries is continuing and must not be interfered with by expressions of hostility and outside menace. Although in the United States there is also some opinion that would seek to encourage such "liberalization," somewhat different policy conclusions have been drawn from the theoretical evaluation and from subsequent events. Both on the level of theory and of practice these differences have caused a good deal of controversy in Indian-American relations.

Policy Development: United States Policy and the Soviet Union (1945–1950)

If their varying interpretations of communism as a social and economic philosophy were the only issue between

India and the United States in this field, their differences would not figure so large. But in the postwar years these differences have become acutely serious because they have directly influenced each country's approach to the Soviet Union.

In the immediate postwar period, Americans were learning several painful and disillusioning lessons about the Soviet leadership. During the same period most Indians were concentrating almost their entire effort on achieving national independence. They lived quite oblivious of the difficulties that were developing among the members of the Grand Alliance in working out postwar settlements. The growing rift between the United States and the Soviet Union therefore came as a surprise and disappointment to Indian opinion. Because most Americans have lived step by step through the painful development of relations with the Soviet Union, it may be difficult for them to understand how little of this history is known in India.

As a matter of fact, circumstances were such that Indians missed the entire personal experience of frustration and menace that Western leaders underwent at the hands of the Russians during the war and subsequent to the German and Japanese surrenders. While plans were being worked out among the major allies for the common victory and then for the postwar settlements, Indian leaders were, at first, in prison for nationalist activities instead of at the council tables of the nations. Later they were overwhelmed by the many grim developments which followed the birth of India's independence: the uprooting of millions of people from lands where their families had lived for centuries; a rising spiral of communal hatred which did not subside till it had claimed Mahatma Gandhi as its victim; disputes with Pakistan which threatened at any moment to break into a full-scale war; the threat posed by the Razakars and Communists in Hyderabad; the pressing need to integrate over five hundred princely states with the administration of the rest of the country; the hammering out of the details of the new republican constitution. All these and many other developments left little time and inclination for Indian leaders to assess the overbearing and tyrannical actions of the Soviet regime in territories which its armies had brought under supposedly temporary military control. Indeed most Indians are even today hardly aware of the grave considerations that forced the United States, after long hesitation, to abandon its traditional policy of avoiding peacetime military alignments and to take up unprecedented economic and military commitments in Europe and Asia. To make this unexpected development in American foreign policy intelligible to Indian readers, it will be helpful briefly to recapitulate events which are still fresh in the minds of most Americans.

With the coming of the peace the average American expected at least a working arrangement with the Soviet Union to continue. He assumed that the Soviet leaders would join with Britain and America in strengthening peace and promoting postwar recovery, on the basis of mutual respect engendered by the cooperation of the war period. It is true that a few specialists in international affairs had expressed a fear that the "artificial alliance" between the United States and the Soviet Union, an alignment born of wartime necessity, would break up after the removal of the common threat and that the Soviet leadership would revert to its claim of possessing a monopoly of wisdom. They thought it natural as John Foster Dulles, then a private citizen, put it,[2]

. . . that the believers in a free society should feel that their ideals would be unsafe if the world became preponderantly totalitarian and intolerant and that proponents of dictatorship of the proletariat should feel unsafe in an environment of individual freedom.

Be that as it may, to the average American and to the average politician disillusionment came hard. It took a number of serious developments in Eastern Europe and

[2] John C. Campbell, *The United States in World Affairs, 1945–1947* (New York: Harper, for the Council on Foreign Relations, 1947); Preface by John Foster Dulles, p. viii.

in Asia to turn an uneasy suspicion of Soviet intentions into a firm conviction that the Soviet leaders attached little or no importance to their solemn promises and that the directions and goals of aggressive Soviet policy had been deliberately chosen and pursued. In the process, a great many efforts were made by American and British leaders to work out postwar solutions jointly with the Soviet government. At Teheran (1943), Yalta (February 1945) and Potsdam (July-August 1945), Presidents Roosevelt and Truman had worked out with British leaders and with Marshal Stalin a series of arrangements for the political and economic future of European and Asian countries liberated from German and Japanese conquest. Addressing Congress on his return from Yalta, President Roosevelt had pictured a new postwar world order based on cooperation through the United Nations, a world in which aggression and spheres of influence, exclusive alliances and balances of power would be things of the past.

Unfortunately, subsequent events belied this hope. Painful experience gradually convinced the American people and government that the Soviet Union was using the presence of its armies in occupied territories for purposes other than those agreed upon at Yalta and Potsdam. Some indications of Soviet intention were found in the manner in which a Soviet-run government was imposed on Rumania only a few days after the Yalta Conference; in the forceful elimination of non-Communist groups from effective participation in elections in Eastern Europe; in the Soviet establishment by armed force of a separatist movement in the Azerbaijan region of Iran; in the growing military support given to Greek Communist guerrillas by the Bulgarian and Yugoslav Communist regimes; in the pressure on Turkey to surrender to Russia one-fourth of its territory together with control of the Straits; in the stripping of Manchurian industry; and in the Soviet refusal to cooperate in establishing a free and united Korea. Winston Churchill, at the time out of office, was among the first to voice alarm at these events. "Nobody knows," he

said in a speech in Fulton, Missouri, in March 1946,[3]
"what Soviet Russia and its Communist international organizations intend to do in the immediate future, or what
are the limits, if any, to their expansive and proselytizing
tendencies. . . ." The dangers that loomed up as the constant Soviet pressure for expansion became clear were multiplied by the fact that the war had ended with the emergence of two "superpowers:" the Soviet Union and the
United States. Gone were the elasticity and shock-absorbing
quality which had in the past resulted from the existence
of several great powers.

Although Churchill's warning words of 1946 were at
first received with strong criticism in the United States,
Soviet step-by-step expansion and unremitting pressure
gradually caused the American people to re-examine their
assumption that the end of the fighting had actually meant
the beginning of genuine peace. It is important in explaining Indian-American differences to note that this re-
examination took place against the background of certain lessons that most Americans had learned for the first
time in the years immediately preceding Pearl Harbor.
In the 1930's the United States had hardly participated in
issues involving war and peace. As a result the aggressor
nations of that time had, correctly enough, formed the impression that the United States was not willing to risk war
by trying to prevent it through alliances or measures of
collective security. Incorrectly interpreting this American reluctance as weakness, and counting on American in-
action in all contingencies, they had seized the initiative.
The collapse of the French in 1940 and the drastic German
threat to British naval power that followed shocked most
Americans into realizing, however, that they could not
under modern conditions remain indifferent to the conquest of all Europe by an aggressive and totalitarian power,

3 "A Shadow Has Fallen on Europe and Asia," delivered at Westminster College, Fulton, Missouri, March 5, 1946, *Vital Speeches of the Day*, v. 12 (March 15, 1946), p. 331.

since such a conquest would pose a direct threat to the security of the United States and of both Americas.

Looking at Europe from 1945 to 1950 and watching Soviet expansion there, many Americans became convinced that the political changes in the balance of power that were taking place were as great a threat to the security of America and of other free countries as Hitler's aggressions had been. The Soviet Union had tremendous military might and it was the focus of an expanding totalitarian communism that skillfully used the combined tactics of domestic intrigue, infiltration, subversion and military intimidation. Furthermore, the Russian state had for generations pushed for "warm water" outlets and the Soviet Union showed no signs of abandoning this goal, especially since it had achieved control over Eastern and Central Europe and was in a position to exercise pressure against Italy, Greece, Turkey and Iran. The Soviet Union embodied a combination of the relentless pressures of Russian ambitions, a secretive and totalitarian state system, and a Messianic doctrine that proclaimed itself the enemy and "grave-digger" of all differing doctrines and systems and whose proponents boasted that it was destined to triumph over the whole world. This combination presented a formidable threat to non-Soviet societies everywhere and particularly to the United States, which seemed to be the only potentially decisive obstacle to Soviet ambitions.

The urgency of the threat was multiplied by the nature of the modern weapons that had been initiated during the war and then developed further. The increasing range of aircraft as well as the development of atomic and guided missiles finally dispelled whatever shreds of illusion there might have been that the United States could ever again be immune to military or political events that created havoc in other parts of the world. As early as October 1945 [4] President Truman had warned the Congress that

[4] *Documents on American Foreign Relations, 1945–1946*, v. 8 (Princeton, N.J.: Princeton University Press, for the World Peace Foundation, 1948), p. 496.

. . . never again can we count on the luxury of time with which to arm ourselves. In any future war, the heart of the United States would be the enemy's first target. Our geographical security is now gone—gone with the advent of the robot bomb, the rocket, aircraft carriers and modern airborne armies.

These were among the major background factors. In policy terms the Soviet Union's cynical disregard of its pledged word in Eastern Europe and elsewhere was at first interpreted by most American leaders as a genuine misunderstanding of international obligations by "the cloistered, hypersuspicious and doctrine-ridden men of the Kremlin." Gradually however—as the deadlock caused by the Soviet veto in the United Nations continued, as the reparations, atomic energy and peace treaty discussions remained deadlocked, while the Soviet Union expanded its influence—as all this continued, Secretary of State Byrnes began to formulate a new policy based on a combination of "patience and firmness, tolerance and understanding." In its broad aims this policy failed, for it did not lead to a settlement of German and Austrian peace conditions. However, after Byrnes made it clear at the Council of Ministers in November 1946 that he did not intend to continue negotiating endlessly over the treaties with Italy, the Balkan nations and Finland, the Soviet Union allowed them to be completed and signed in February 1947. The treaties as drawn contained more concessions to Soviet than to Western views.

However there was no basic change in Soviet policies or Soviet goals. Therefore when news came from London that Britain's grave economic situation would force it to discontinue economic and military support to Greece and Turkey after March 1947, the United States faced a vital decision: could it, in terms of its own security and that of Western Europe and West Asia, allow Communist pressures on Greece and Turkey to bring them under Soviet domination or should it take the unprecedented step of assuming the responsibilities toward these countries the

British had hitherto borne? Addressing the Congress on March 12,[5] President Truman advocated a new policy, that of containment:

I believe that it must be the policy of the United States to support free peoples who are resisting attempted subjugation by armed minorities or by outside pressures. I believe that we must assist free peoples to work out their own destinies in their own way.

During the searching debate on the Greek and Turkish Aid bill which followed, the late Senator Arthur H. Vandenberg, Chairman of the Senate Foreign Relations Committee and a former spokesman of the isolationist wing of the Republican party, supported the President's plea: [6]

. . . I think we should . . . face it very, very frankly, because I do not know that there is any alternative. . . . when you have a type of government which is given over to expansion through all history so long as that expansion can succeed and grow, and there is no limit to its growth until some other counterforce opposes it. . . .

The Congress accepted the President's plea and aid to Greece and Turkey was granted.

In the meantime it was becoming increasingly clear that acute danger in Europe was not confined to Greece and Turkey. A very bad harvest in Western Europe in 1946, followed by an extremely cold winter, had intensified the pressure on its exhausted domestic economies and its depleted foreign exchange resources. There were not enough necessities of life to go around. Goods which used to pay for the import of materials to supplement local resources did not exist and could not be produced without imported materials. Although the United States had since V-E Day provided $11,000,000,000 through UNRRA, and other grants of supplies (including $465,000,000 to the

[5] *Documents on American Foreign Relations, 1947,* v. 9 (1949), cited, p. 7.

[6] *Assistance to Greece and Turkey,* Hearings before the U.S. Senate Committee on Foreign Relations on S. 938, 80th Cong., 1st Sess. (Washington: GPO, 1947), p. 75.

Soviet Union), through loans and private donations to European countries, this help had not corrected the underlying causes of Europe's distress.

To American eyes there were many signs that the Soviet leaders saw in this postwar exhaustion a unique opportunity for establishing Russian supremacy over all of Europe simply by obstructing any efforts at economic recovery and political settlement. American leaders feared that, if the forces of disintegration were allowed to work unchecked, the political and economic institutions of Western Europe would collapse and local Communist parties would capture power everywhere. Then—without having fired a shot—the Soviet Union would dominate the vast expanse of territory from the Pacific to the Atlantic, a territory containing a large population, much of the industry of the world and much of its resources. Such an eventuality would, they felt, expose the United States to incalculable risks that could not be accepted.

Without heavy American aid Europe's economic ills could not be cured. Secretary of State Marshall in June 1947 quietly suggested that the European nations jointly prepare a program of economic reconstruction on the basis of which the United States could then determine what aid it could afford to give to Europe as a whole. In developing his proposal Marshall was careful to explain that the American policy was "directed not against any country or doctrine, but against hunger, poverty, desperation and chaos." Although the American experience with Soviet maneuvers in the distribution of UNRRA aid had not been a happy one and although the postwar development of Soviet policy had been a great disappointment to American opinion, still no European nations were excluded from Secretary Marshall's proposal.

It was in fact the Soviet leadership that rejected the proffered aid and that forbade its satellites to accept it. Three weeks after Marshall's speech Molotov came to Paris, supposedly to discuss the necessary arrangements with the British and French Foreign Ministers. But Molotov was adamant that each country draw up its own requirements and negotiate separately for aid with the United States. The East European countries under Soviet domination—even those that had shown a very active interest—were thereupon also faced by a Soviet demand that they have nothing to do with the Marshall Plan. By its action the Soviet Union prevented the formulation of an all-European program of recovery and cooperation and gave a further strong impetus to the process by which Europe was being broken into two camps.

While the sixteen West European countries were working out the details of their economic cooperation, Communist leaders from nine European countries met in Poland and revived in slightly disguised form the prewar Communist International, now renamed the Communist Information Bureau (Cominform). At this meeting Soviet Politburo member Andrei Zhdanov also launched an all-out attack on the Marshall Plan as an attempt to establish a "protectorate" over Europe. Following the meeting widespread strikes in France and Italy—which had the largest Communist parties of Western Europe—threatened to develop into civil war; it was in these countries that the Communist efforts to sabotage the Marshall Plan were concentrated. At the same time the Soviet Union consolidated further its control of Eastern Europe through the quick conclusion of treaties of military aid and alliance with the Communist-imposed governments of Bulgaria, Rumania and Hungary along the lines of its exclusive treaties concluded in 1945 with Poland and Yugoslavia.

These developments—especially when coupled with a Communist coup in Czechoslovakia in February 1948 and the accidental death or murder of Jan Masaryk, son of the founder of the Czechoslovak Republic—aroused great anxiety in Western Europe and the United States. Many people wondered openly whether Austria, Italy or France was next on the Soviet list. By March 1948 these events provoked Secretary Marshall to comment that the situation was "disturbingly similar" to that in the years before 1939 when the Nazis had threatened to overrun Europe. On March 29 President Truman warned that certain things were worse than war, one of them being slavery. "That's what we were faced with in 1940 and 1941. We are," he said, "faced with almost exactly the same situation today." It was in this atmosphere of anxiety that the American Congress on March 31, 1948, passed the European Recovery Program through which $17,000,000,000 were to be channeled into the recovery of Western Europe over the next four years.

Meanwhile in Europe this alarm had earlier in the same month culminated in the signing by France, Britain, Belgium, the Netherlands and Luxembourg of the so-called Brussels Pact. The core of the agreement—which was to last fifty years—lay in the promise to give "all military and other aid and assistance in [each signatory's] power" to any one of the signatories whose territory or armed forces might be the object of an armed attack in Europe. A permanent Consultative Council was set up to deal with all questions that might arise under the treaty. Together with another regional pact, the Rio Treaty of 1947 for the mutual defense of the twenty American republics, the Brussels Pact formed the precedent for the North Atlantic Treaty.

In June 1948 the Soviet leadership opened another chapter in its effort to dominate all of Europe when it startled the world by blocking surface traffic coming into West Berlin by land or water. This posed a crisis of the first magnitude to the British, French and American governments, which shared with the Soviet Union in the four-power administration of that city, and which were suddenly faced with the alternatives of withdrawing from Berlin and abandoning its people to Soviet rule, or of transporting massive quantities of fuel, food and other necessities to sustain life and hope in the 2,500,000 citizens of West Berlin. One alternative open to them was to force traffic lanes through Soviet-occupied territory to reach Berlin—a course that ran the grave risk of leading to war. Instead, the Western powers set out with quiet determination to launch an aircraft operation unparalleled even in time of war. Working round the clock, in 318 days their airmen flew more than 1,500,000 tons of supplies over Soviet-controlled territory into West Berlin.

It was during these critical and anxious days that public opinion in Western countries was driven to the conclusion that the only argument the Soviet leadership recognized and respected was that of alert resourcefulness and military preparedness. Clearly, it was the presence of Western troops in Berlin as a token of the will to resist and the availability of personnel and planes that had enabled the Western powers to parry the Soviet attempt to seize the whole of Berlin by starvation. The conviction grew in the United States that economic assistance to Western Europe was not by itself enough to meet the existing threats. On January 14, 1949, after months of discussions with the Brussels Treaty states, the Department of State affirmed that "formal association of the United States with these countries in an arrangement directed against aggression evidently will be needed." On April 4, 1949, the North Atlantic Treaty was signed by ten Western European countries and by Canada and the United States. Each signatory pledged itself to maintain and develop the capacity to resist armed attack, to consult together in the event of threats, and to regard an armed attack against one or more as an attack against all. Largely because of the American constitutional structure the NATO agreement did not have the automatic character of the Brussels Pact but provided that assistance to any signatory attacked should involve "such actions as [each signatory] deems necessary, including the use of armed force, to restore and maintain the security of the North Atlantic area." Supplementary bilateral agreements were worked out with European members of the North Atlantic community during the course of the year and by March 1950 the Defense Committee of the Organization had drawn up a plan for the integrated protection of Western Europe.

Until it joined in creating NATO, the United States

had never taken part in a system of European alliances. Even in 1917 and 1941 the word "alliance" had been avoided in favor of euphemisms to describe collaboration with other countries. As late as 1947, when the United States was becoming fearful that the Soviet leaders were aiming to take over Europe, it had not remobilized its largely disbanded armies; it had simply indicated that its policy was to stand firm and not allow further extension of the advances which Soviet power had made in Europe between 1945 and 1947. The decision to create a system of mutual defense was taken only after the Russians had exploded their first atomic bomb and after a prolonged and vigorous public debate which extended far beyond the walls of the Capitol at Washington. It was with evident reluctance that the people of the United States assumed the heavy burden of unparalleled economic assistance and military support to Western Europe. This policy of banding together in a defensive coalition was not meant to shut the door against future negotiations; it was taken in the hope that situations of weakness might be replaced by positions of strength so that "they can be recognized and out of them can grow agreement." Speaking on March 16, 1950,[7] Secretary of State Acheson explained:

Our attitude is not inflexible, our opinions are not frozen. . . . We are always ready to discuss, to negotiate, to agree, but we are understandably loath to play the role of international sucker. We will take the initiative in the future as we have in the past in seeking agreement whenever there is any indication that this course would be a fruitful one.

Indian Evaluation of Soviet Goals

It was at about this time that the leaders of the young Indian Republic—having overcome many serious domestic difficulties—were able to look around and take note of what had happened in the West. By then the division of

[7] "Tensions between the United States and the Soviet Union," speech at the University of California (Berkeley), *Department of State Bulletin,* v. 22 (March 27, 1950), p. 477.

Europe into two military camps had taken shape and the great debate in the United States was mainly over. Most Indians had been remote from the atmosphere of crisis created by the provocative steps of the Soviet Union as well as unaware of the evident reluctance with which the United States had adjusted its historic attitude toward Europe and brought it into line with the new realities of the international scene. What Indians saw was the close military association of the United States with the colonial powers of Western Europe. Not enough people outside India have realized the impact of this association on Indian thinking.

Throughout their long history Indians have had little direct contact with the Russians. There had been nothing in India's national experience to give specific content to the Western picture of the Soviet leadership and its international Communist movement as insatiably aggressive and a threat to the independence of nations and to human freedom. Differences in personal experience also counted for a great deal here. While millions of Americans are related by descent and common tradition to the victims of Communist oppression in Eastern Europe and the Soviet Union, there have been no similarities linking Indians with the misfortunes of these people—about whom they have until very recently been generally uninformed. Rather, Indian opinion has been impressed by the Soviet Union's long-term propaganda support for anticolonialism and in particular by its well-publicized support to the freedom movements in Indonesia, Indochina and Malaya. It has correspondingly been irritated by the United States' commitment of financial and military support to allies who in their role as colonial powers were trying to crush nationalist resistance. This view of American policy in Europe tended to destroy the earlier oversimplified Indian image of the United States as an international knight-errant of liberty. The suspicion and distrust with which the Indians viewed the policies of colonial powers were gradually extended to include the United States. As a result the American role in helping Indonesia to its independence has not been appreciated nor have its efforts at assistance in other Asian areas.

Apart from a natural rejection of colonialism and a generally favorable appraisal of the theory of Soviet rule, and also of Soviet industrial achievements, the foundations of the Indian attitude toward the Soviet Union are to be found in the Indian evaluation of the Soviet-United States conflict since 1945 and its effect on Asia. Since independence India has been subjected to intensive propaganda efforts from both sides in the conflict. Their net effect in India has been a widely accepted view of the conflict as basically a clash of power rather than of ideals and one in which the key area was a remote Europe rather than Asia. Both these conclusions have encouraged India to fight shy of involvement in the cold war.

Indian leaders have thus declined to accept a black and white "cold war" picture of postwar developments that asserted the presence of right on one side exclusively. Furthermore, when the United States interpreted the Soviet threat in moral terms, leading Indians suggested that Americans had not argued thus during the Litvinov period of Soviet diplomacy nor during the wartime alliance. The American retort that during the Litvinov period the Soviet Union had given the impression of intending to act according to accepted international standards and that—as far as the war period was concerned—in a war for national survival the leaders of any nation must seek allies wherever they can, made little impression on Indian opinion. Most leaders of Indian thought have also concluded that the Soviet Union feared American intentions at least as much as the United States feared Soviet intentions. In support of this conclusion they point to the Soviet emphasis on United States participation in the international intervention after the Bolshevik revolution. They point also to the postwar Russian fears of American atomic weapons and to the complaints of Soviet leaders after World War II concerning American "aggressive" designs.

Thus, after the Western nations had organized themselves into NATO, it appeared to many Indians to be a barren controversy whether the Soviet Union was driven by ambition or fear or both; fear was evidently present on both sides, they thought, as Europe was divided between competing and hostile alliances.

Looking to Asia, Indian leaders have interpreted the Communist threat as coming from within Asian societies rather than from Soviet military aggression. What would be the need or the advantage for the Soviet Union, Indians ask, in attacking a country in South or Southeast Asia? Asia is spread over a large area and is industrially underdeveloped; occupation of Asian countries would—so the argument runs—hardly add to Soviet military strength.

Here lies one of the direct differences in the appraisals of Soviet policies that carry the most weight in India and in the United States. Simplified for the purposes of argument, the prevailing Indian view has been that the Soviet program for Asia rests on political, cultural and economic penetration rather than on military conquest. It would follow that the Communists' best gambit is to infiltrate the ranks of Asian political parties for their own purposes. In Asia the Communist appeal has not been in terms of the overawing force of Soviet armed might—its atomic weapons and huge armies and air power—but in terms of ending colonialism and of promoting economic plenty through drastic land reforms, collectivized agriculture and nationalized industry. This appeal has been directed not at the strategic fears but at the aspirations of governments as well as at the common man and his hopes. Therefore, many Indians would say, Americans have misread the significance of Asian Communist movements because—as Indians see it—they have thought of Communists as conspiratorial gamblers for power rather than as leaders who offer answers, which may be honest or misleading, to some of the pressing questions facing Asian peoples. By talking of the Communist danger to the free world, of which the ordinary people in Asia have no conception, and by stressing the importance of military alliances and underemphasizing social and economic measures, the United States is in this Indian view leaving the social and economic back door wide open to subversion while guarding the military front gate against an unlikely overt Soviet aggression.

This analysis is bound to disturb American opinion, chiefly for three reasons. In the prevalent American view it is first of all impossible to answer categorically the question of the direction Soviet policy might or might not have taken in the absence of military alliances such as NATO, the Baghdad Pact or SEATO. The Soviet Union after all encouraged the use of military force in Asia, as in Korea and in Indochina, and threatened to use it against Berlin, Turkey and Yugoslavia. It is not that the American government discounts the major danger that arises from the possibility of Soviet and Chinese Communist infiltration of all types. Far from it. The American government feels, nevertheless, that a military "umbrella," no matter how symbolic, extended over parts of the area serves as notice of an active American concern and makes open military action by the Communists more risky for them and therefore more unlikely.

The second reason why the Indian analysis given above would be disturbing to most American opinion is in the picture of the Communist which it gives. In the prevalent American view, thinking of the Communist as primarily a hard-working reformer of good will misses much of the significance of the role of the Moscow-oriented party man. In the American view, the international Communist apparatus has demonstrated time and again that it has many arms and utilizes many different types of workers whom it trains according to their several functions. The Communist plan thus has its uses for the propagandist who works among the people, for the dedicated and disciplined member of a secret cadre, for the spy and organizer, for the "united front" man of conciliation and for the fellow traveler. It is impossible to assess Communist world strategy without considering all varieties of its tactical application.

Finally, the Indian analysis given above would perturb American opinion because it shows so clearly that Americans have failed to communicate to the majority of informed Indians what the United States has done and is trying to do in Asia. There appears to have been too much talk of military aid and too little of the emergency shipments of food, programs of agricultural reform and of technical and economic assistance which the United States has initiated or promoted in Asia. Criticism of the United States for causing higher defense expenditures in some Asian countries through its programs in other Asian countries, along with the criticism that the United States has ignored the need for economic development and has misread Asian experience since 1945, indicate how serious has been this failure in communication. It should not be impossible to remedy this and to promote a better understanding of American policies among wider groups of people in India.

In sum, for the reasons already outlined, as well as because of the influences of geographic location and power position, the Indian government and people have been far more concerned with the dangers of war which arise from the great split in Europe than with the rights and wrongs of its origin. As a result they have refused to take any public stand on the causes of the European conflict or on questions of right and wrong in that conflict and have confined themselves to pointing out the dangers involved in the building up of military blocs and the piling up of armaments by both sides and to pleading for general disarmament. This approach has been criticized in the United States, in the Soviet Union and elsewhere as failing to make vital distinctions. Some small groups in India—among them the Praja Socialists—have protested that the government's reluctance to pronounce on the responsibility of postwar Soviet policies for intensifying European tensions or to understand and support the position of

major free countries both jeopardize Indian security and
repudiate India's responsibility to act as a leading Asian
nation. Official policy has, however, continued to receive
strong public backing because it fits the over-all Indian
view of the cold war and of India's role in seeking to lessen its dangers.

The Indian "Bridge" Policy

Indians are generally aware—though most foreigners
probably are not—that the ways in which India seeks to influence the great powers stem directly from the methods
by which India's nationalists won its independence from
British rule. Rather than attempt the hopeless task of opposing Britain's forces with arms, Indian nationalists under Mahatma Gandhi's leadership emphasized the building up of political consciousness and self-confidence among
the masses through the tactics of *satyagraha*. *Satyagraha*
pressure is nonviolent. It has the advantage of always leaving the door open to further negotiations. It was effective
when applied against the British, although it may be de-
bated whether its success was due to the reasonableness of
the British rather than to some inherent capacity to exert
irresistible pressure against any opponent.

When India became independent in a world which was
already split, the new goal was to prevent any outbreak
of hostilities among the major powers. Acutely conscious
of India's slender industrial base and its widespread poverty, the government felt that it could not hope to meet
international challenges by military means but believed
that it might contribute to defending world peace by
steadily pressing nonviolent and conciliatory proposals
aimed at bridging the chasm between the anti-Communist
powers and the Soviet bloc. Thus the way of the *Pancha
Shil* became its policy: five principles of state conduct to
seek peace through peaceful means. Indians already had
deep-rooted ideological, institutional, and economic links
with the Western democracies. To pursue its "bridge" pol-

icy, the Indian government consciously strove to build up friendly relations with Communist countries as well, even though it rejected their political ideology. It also deliberately refrained from criticizing their systems of administration or domestic development. A considerable portion of Indian opinion followed the government's lead, arguing that criticism of the Soviet Union and its partners was unlikely to do any good while it would interfere with India's effort to play the uncommitted middleman of good will toward both blocs.

In the United States and among small groups in India the charge has on occasion nevertheless been made that the Indian government has not held an even balance and that it has criticized the Western nations while refraining from criticizing the Soviet Union. This appears to the critics of Indian policy as using different-colored spectacles to look at the United States and the Soviet Union. Against this it is argued that Indian leaders feel freer to criticize Western countries partly because they are closer to them and more friendly with them and can therefore perhaps hope to have greater influence with them, and partly because many Western measures directly involve Indian interests, whereas Indian leaders see no direct threats to India from Communist aggression. The argument that Indian security will be directly affected should that of its Western friends be destroyed by Communist aggression seems to have little impact on the Indian outlook. That this difference in outlook remains an irritant in Indian-American relations is generally recognized.

The Indian policy of nonalignment has attracted the support of several Asian governments and the enthusiasm of large numbers of people, particularly in non-Communist parts of Asia and in parts of Africa. It has imparted a considerable authority to India's voice in international affairs far outweighing India's military strength. So long as vital world problems can be approached peacefully, India has a conspicuous role to play as a spokesman for a resurgent Asia and as a mediator. Thus, the world situation toward which Indian policy strives is one in which force as a factor in international affairs will be reduced to the absolute minimum and no concentrations of power built up around the militarily strong nations. It is in this situation that India's influence could be at a maximum of effectiveness.

Politics conducted by power blocs leaves India with little elbowroom in which to play the mediator. Any use of violence around its perimeter threatens it both directly and indirectly because it pushes the adjacent countries involved to join one or another of the power blocs and thus brings the forces of the great powers back into portions of the world surrounding India. Indians fear that if weaker nations, including India, are organized under military pacts they will be reduced to playing the puppet to stronger nations. To all these developments India is diametrically opposed, for its goal is to be surrounded by a series of states which will be independent of all outside power (including, if possible, even a China wholly independent of Russia). Among these states, India, the strongest except China, would then hope to give at least ideological and moral leadership. The tendency of Indian policy in Asia is to seek at almost any price some sort of tranquillity based on a congeries of autonomous and unallied states. In such a situation economic development of the Asian states could proceed unmolested by outside forces or world rivalries. Hence, there is little motivation for India to align itself with the anti-Communist alliance or with the Soviet bloc. Nonalignment expresses well the mixed feelings of Indians toward the two sides in the conflict. It also fits the strategy which India is following of engaging in a maximum of political activity without having corresponding military power. Thanks to the persistence of the deadlocked balance of the two blocs, India can negotiate with both sides, assuming the outward mien of authority though lacking the usual tools of power.

Military Pacts in Indian-United States Relations

The United States and India, as we have seen, look upon the Soviet Union from widely differing angles. This divergence has led them to disagree sharply over several issues, prominent among them being the matter of military pacts. This is an issue that touches the national interests of both, challenges their deepest beliefs concerning the best way they can help the cause of peace, and arouses deep emotional sensitivities. It has been largely responsible for one of the gravest developments in Indian-American relations to date. It underlies the belief, held in many popular circles and also in some powerful groups within each country, that the other government's policies are not only misconceived but also harmful to the common aim of securing peace and freedom for all nations. No attempt to improve Indian-American relations can hope for success unless it faces frankly the issue of military pacts.

We have seen in brief how NATO was formed. Indians did not particularly object to NATO as a European defense system. They did protest that it had the indirect effect of strengthening metropolitan powers against which Asian nationalist groups were struggling. And they objected even more vigorously when another system of joint defense arrangements was extended by the United States to various countries in Asia, particularly to Pakistan.

In Europe and America, NATO—under the umbrella of the American capability for atomic retaliation—was widely credited with having saved Western Europe from Soviet aggression. Western Europe however was not the only threatened area. Events from 1949 on persuaded the leaders of a number of countries in Asia, Europe and America that the Soviet leadership—having been blocked in the West—was turning its eyes eastward. Aggression launched from North Korea, guerrilla warfare in Indochina and increased Soviet activities from Afghanistan to the Arab countries all suggested efforts to probe the vulnerabilities of the non-Communist countries. These Soviet tactics caused alarm in many countries which feared that they might be consumed in local "brushfire" wars in a situation which was in the large moving toward stalemate. At first the United States was reluctant to expand its already large military commitments. But in 1951 the United States joined in pacts of mutual defense with Australia and New Zealand and with the Philippine Republic, and later with Japan, South Korea and the Chinese Nationalists in Formosa. In 1954 it made a military assistance agreement with Pakistan. And after the Communists' success in taking over North Viet Nam, the United States in September 1954 took a leading part in organizing the Southeast Asia Treaty Organization. In 1955 it also encouraged the expansion of the Turko-Iraqi treaty into the five-nation Baghdad Pact, without itself fully joining it. This policy seemed a logical and necessary extension of the over-all pattern of military containment and of holding out the threat of American reprisal as a deterrent to Communist aggression. By strengthening and stiffening the forces of its allies the United States also sought to meet the criticism that reliance on the Strategic Air Force for massive retaliation would not stop the outbreak of local aggressions similar to the attack on South Korea.

To most Indians this policy is open to several objections which seem to them so strong as to invalidate its basic premises. First of all, most Indians accept as an article of faith the view that there is little or no danger of Soviet armed aggression in Asia. The very establishment of military alliances along the fringe of the Soviet Union and China, they argue, makes it likely that these nations will take counteractions. Such alliances therefore by their very existence increase the chances of war. Most American estimates hold, on the contrary, that the Soviet leadership is more likely to push into power vacuums than into areas where it is bound to meet with strong opposition. This is an issue on which neither side appears able to persuade the other to its view.

One difference between the Indian and American views on the menace of communism, a difference which in turn leads to contrary views on the effect of military pacts, appears to result from what might be called their time perspectives. Indians often express a confidence that with time and patience the Communist regimes will mellow and soften. When queried they often indicate that the period of time required for this might run to several decades. Few Americans are likely to be satisfied with a policy that does not hold out a prospect of improvement for the next two decades or more. At home Indians are more concerned than Americans with what may happen in the next five years during which India will be carrying out its crucial development plans. In foreign policy it is the American view that certain strategic precautions taken now, even at some risk, will pay off by opening the path to a better settlement a decade or two hence. Indian policy is more concerned with peace here and now and is unwilling to participate in these steps or shoulder any part of the risk. To a number of Americans it appears that this policy undoubtedly relieves anxiety in Moscow and Peking to some degree and enables them to take a more relaxed, less hurried, stance. In the American view Indian policy may to that extent pay off in the short run. But what if, as Americans believe, the drive to communize the world is in reality fiercely adhered to by the Communist powers and over the coming decades the Soviet Union continues to seize opportunities, one by one, to undermine or conquer countries which fall into difficulties? How then will a policy of nonalignment and independent action secure India, or any other nation, from eventually finding itself surrounded by overwhelming Communist power? The Socialists and many independents in India have asked the same question, but to most Indians this possibility represents a less immediate and less frightening danger than the nuclear war which they believe to be the logical outcome of continued American-Soviet antagonism.

Coexistence and the Hungarian Crisis

Since the Nineteenth Party Congress of 1952, and even more since 1955, the Soviet leadership has laid great stress on prospects of "coexistence" between the Communist powers and the democracies. Premier Bulganin and Nikita Khrushchev dwelt on this theme during their spectacular tour through India in the winter of 1955–1956. Although the Soviet leaders' castigation of Stalin and his rule shook certain longstanding Indian preconceptions about the Soviet Union and other Communist regimes, many highly placed Indians were nevertheless impressed when spokesmen at the Twentieth Communist Party Congress in 1956 announced that the Soviet leaders had ended the "cult of the individual" and were widening the distribution of political power to protect the people by more effective checks on the government; that war between Communist states and other states was not inevitable; that there were several roads to socialism; and that "coexistence" was possible. When Prime Minister Nehru observed that "they are moving toward great changes from which they will not be able to turn back," he gave the lead to a new Indian assessment of the Soviet Union.

This optimistic assessment differs considerably from the prevailing American view. Although some American observers occasionally discern a gleam of hope that a genuine and irreversible process of "liberalization," a process that could lead to an honorable and lasting peace for the non-Communist world, has begun, Americans generally feel it safer to adopt an attitude of "wait and see." Nor do they feel that the Soviet arguments at the Twentieth Communist Party Congress have been thoroughly convincing. They remember, for example, that even in the recent past the Soviet leadership has shown itself a master of the quick change in tactics; and, furthermore, that the new policies, as the Soviet spokesmen have themselves emphasized, have their antecedents in the Lenin and Stalin periods and might be subject to the abrupt reversals which have taken place in the Soviet Union in the past. In addition, some Americans point out that in justifying the new policies, Soviet leaders have indicated a number of international strategic reasons which made war less likely. And, in discussing the Soviet statement that socialism need not come elsewhere as it had in Russia, Americans have been struck by the fact that there is no evidence of Soviet change in goal, but only in method. As for coexistence, the Soviet statement pointed out merely that there must be an interim period before world revolution could be achieved, during which Socialist and non-Socialist states would both exist. Such an analysis did not in American eyes indicate any intention to abandon long-term Communist goals and gave American policy-makers no good reason for slackening their effort to keep America's defenses strong.

It was Nehru's point however that even though the ultimate Communist goals might remain unchanged the statement did, so he believed, express a real anxiety on the part of Soviet leaders to relax international tensions. He felt that this trend should be encouraged. Thus the *rapprochement* between Tito and Soviet leaders as well as the relaxation of Soviet controls over Poland were welcomed in India not only for their own sake but as signs of a more relaxed trend in Soviet policy. Later indications that these developments had in large part been only temporary were accepted as setbacks in what was nevertheless regarded as a basic process of liberalization which, once started, was likely to continue in the absence of any overwhelming menace from outside. As compared to earlier interpretations, however, the Indian acceptance of new and benign Soviet claims contained a certain element of caution.

Widespread Indian skepticism of Soviet policies first emerged during the Hungarian crisis of late 1956. The popular rising in Hungary, coming as it did just before the Israeli attack and the Anglo-French intervention in Egypt, was at first not widely understood within India. But the reaction was not long in coming. While the government moved with hesitation and caution, large segments of Indian opinion condemned Soviet intervention in forthright terms. When the Indian government vehemently condemned Britain, France and Israel but refrained from criticizing the Soviet intervention and on November 9, 1956, voted against the widely supported United Nations resolution condemning the Soviet Union, it was severely criticized for the first time in Indian political circles and in the Indian press for applying a double standard. The government's expressed concern over the return of Soviet troops to Hungary within two or three days after the Soviet government had promised to withdraw them and its distress at their intervention "in the civil conflict" did not satisfy its critics at home. The strength of popular criticism was reflected in the debates in Parliament that took place during November. In an official pronouncement the Prime Minister explained the initial caution as due to lack of reliable information. He justified India's vote in the United Nations on the ground that the Indian government was opposed not to the entire resolution but only to a clause recommending United Nations supervision of Hungarian elections. Furthermore, he continued, condemnation of the Soviet action, even by the United Nations, would not help secure the withdrawal of Soviet troops. Soviet leaders, feeling they were besieged by the Western alliances, he said, would hardly respond to United Nations pressure. He was afraid the Hungarian situation might touch off a world war. He had called for United Nations action against Britain and France because he expected that it would be effective. Thereafter the Prime Minister, both on his own and in association with the Prime Ministers of Burma, Ceylon and Indonesia, called for a speedy withdrawal of Soviet forces from Hungary and urged that the Hungarian people be left free to decide on their own form of government and their relations with the Soviet Union without any outside pressure or interference.

In contrast to India, the American government and people reacted strongly in both the Egyptian and the Hungarian crises. President Eisenhower, who called the Anglo-French action an "act of aggression," supported vigorous measures both in the United Nations and outside to meet both crises. Notwithstanding Indian official hesitations, a considerable body of Indian public opinion had responded to the Hungarian issue on lines similar to American opinion and the Indian government's subsequent position on Hungary—which accepted the fighting in Hungary as a national rising—also came closer to the American response to Soviet action.

Reactions to the Hungarian crisis did not, of course, erase Indian-American differences over their interpretations of Soviet intentions. Given the positions and outlooks that have been considered in this chapter, it seems unlikely that India and the United States can soon or easily come together in a mutually satisfying policy toward the Soviet Union. Yet, Indian reactions to the Soviet exposures of the nature of Stalin's rule and to the Hungarian crisis may signal a new period during which Indians will feel less inhibited about judging Soviet actions as severely as they do those of the Western nations. Such a development would greatly improve Indian-American relations. It would obviate the temptation to question each other's good faith and might lead to more realistic mutual appraisals of Soviet policies.

Chapter 4

PAKISTAN IN INDIAN-AMERICAN
RELATIONS

NEXT ONLY to the problem of international communism, it is differences over policies toward Pakistan which have brought misunderstandings and irritation into Indian-American relations. To some observers the Indian attitude toward Pakistan seems somewhat comparable to the American attitude toward the Soviet Union. Just as the United States has come to view the aims of the Soviet leadership as the greatest threat to its security, so India looks on Pakistan as the main threat to its security. Among the many factors that have gone into the formation of these attitudes—and which have already been mentioned—it is worthwhile to point out here the effect of the refugee movements in both countries. Thus in recent years Indian images of Pakistan have been powerfully affected by the stories of some millions of refugees from Pakistan, just as American images of the Soviet tyranny have been influenced by the accounts of refugees from Soviet Russia and from Communist-ruled states of Eastern Europe.

It is true also that American responses to Indian-Pakistan friction have, at times, been reminiscent of Indian responses to Soviet-American friction. When it comes to India and Pakistan, it is the United States which seeks friendly relations with both countries, and which explores ways of bringing them closer together while itself trying not to take sides in their disputes. Americans have deplored what they consider to be the stiffness of Indian attitudes toward Pakistan, just as Indians have in the same way deplored the stiffness of American attitudes toward the Soviet Union. These comparisons do not of course give a full picture of Indian-American differences over Pakistan, but they do suggest that in considering problems of relations between India and the United States we have to take into account differences in perspective as well as in applying principles.

The difference in perspective from which India and the United States approach Pakistan is clear and sharp. India lives with memories of the partition of the Indian subcontinent in 1947, when widespread communal fighting and mass migrations heightened the social and political tensions that had been generated during the independence movement. Both governments avowed their desire for friendly relations. Even under the most peaceable of conditions it would have been difficult to solve amicably the problems of dividing assets formerly held in common, deciding on the equitable use of waters jointly held in the past, dividing military stores, dealing with the problems focused on the resettlement of the refugees, with severed trade ties and with a host of other troublesome issues. The boiling animosities of 1947, when combined with the tensions and suspicions that developed from the failure of the princes of Hyderabad, Junagadh and Kashmir to accede to either new state before the formal advent of freedom, inevitably increased the difficulties in the way of their solution.

Although some uneven progress has been registered, several of the major disputes between India and Pakistan have remained unresolved. Their persistence has deepened the frustration, distrust and anxiety that have marked India's approach to Pakistan. Inevitably India's continuing anxiety about Pakistan and the emotional tension between the two countries have affected Indian estimates of American policies toward Pakistan.

The United States for its part welcomed equally the advent of both Pakistan and India in 1947. Americans hoped that partition, since it had been accepted as unavoidable by both sides, would help resolve the tensions that had loomed increasingly large as independence approached. They hoped too that after the partition disturbances were over both countries would achieve national progress, stability and cooperation in an atmosphere of increasing friendliness. It seemed clear to Americans that both countries would profit from such a change. It was further hoped that if peace and stability developed in this important area there would be fewer pretexts for outside meddling and subversion.

Having no reasons for being unfriendly with either country, the United States has repeatedly expressed its desire, wherever possible, to help each country to develop and strengthen itself. Both India and Pakistan have received economic help from the United States. American military help and political alliance have gone to Pakistan only and not also to India solely because India has declined such help and association. Where the United States has had to take positions inside or outside the United Nations on Indian-Pakistan quarrels—as in the case of Kashmir—it has according to its own lights made every effort to judge the issues on their merits in an attempt to help the two countries bridge the differences between them.

The divergent Indian and American perspectives have found their way into policies which—because they touch immediate security interests—have caused intense reactions. Kashmir and the American military aid program in Pakistan are the two prime examples. The differences here are real. The question is whether—without doing violence to the essential interests of either—India and the United States can find a closer adjustment of their respective policies.

Pakistan plainly occupies a very different position in the security plans of India from its place in the security plans of America. Although American security is involved to the degree that Pakistan is part of the "ring of deterrence," the United States neither fears Pakistan nor regards Pakistan as likely to commit aggression. Its interest in the Kashmir dispute derives from its general desire to strengthen peace and justice. For India, on the other hand, Pakistan is an immediate neighbor that both commands the major and traditional invasion route into India from the northwest and that is considered as having been an aggressor in Kashmir. This estimate of danger to vital Indian interests has resulted in a pronounced emotional strain, a mounting burden on the Indian national budget, and continuing bad relations with a close neighbor in other aspects of their relations as well. The Indian desire to limit Pakistan influence has also affected some aspects of India's broader international policy, such as—in the American view—its diplomacy in West Asia. It has furthermore, at least to some Americans, seemed to make India more willing to accept Soviet political support and has possibly served to inhibit the official Indian reaction to the Soviet military suppression of the Hungarian uprising in November 1956. It should be added that these interpretations are sharply questioned in India.

The Kashmir Problem

Within this context let us turn first to the Kashmir dispute, not to examine the details of India's quarrel with Pakistan but to isolate those factors in the case that have in the past exacerbated Indian-American relations and that continue to do so. Particularly important in 1957 was the Indian position that the United States has consistently misinterpreted the Kashmir situation from the time it was introduced before the Security Council in January 1948. Then India, in a complaint under Article 35, Chapter 6 of the Charter (dealing with the pacific settlement of disputes), requested that the Council ask the government of Pakistan to prevent its official personnel—military and civil—from participating or assisting in the invasion of Jammu and Kashmir State; to call upon other Pakistan nationals to desist from taking any part in the fighting in that state; and to deny to the invaders access to and use of its territory for operations against Kashmir, for passage of military and other supplies, and for all other kinds of aid that might tend to prolong the struggle.

In his complaint the Indian representative described in detail the burnings, lootings and murders carried out by the invaders as they swept down into Kashmir. These activities had led the Indian government to take military action. He also recounted the encouragement and assistance —all but formally official—that the invaders (comprising nationals of Pakistan and tribesmen from immediately adjoining territories had received and were still receiving from Pakistan. India had accepted the Maharaja's urgent request for accession to India on October 26, 1947. Therefore India felt it was acting within Indian territory, and that the acts of lawlessness and worse were taking place in India. Because of the accession, the aid which the invaders were receiving from Pakistan constituted an act of aggression against India. The Indian delegate also stressed the special urgency of the Security Council's taking immediate action; otherwise, the government of India in military action undertaken against the invaders might be compelled in self-defense to enter Pakistan.

No such urgent action by the Security Council was forthcoming and it was the so-called "broad and human" Pakistan presentation of practically all issues between India and Pakistan that received the Council's attention rather than the so-called more limited and "legalistic" complaint presented by India on the Kashmir situation. Indians could not in these circumstances help feeling that the Security Council did not understand the Indian position or realize why the Indian government had not made a straight charge of aggression against Pakistan under Chapter 7 of the Charter. From the Indian point of view, nothing could have been gained by exacerbating the issue by asking the United Nations to condemn Pakistan as an aggressor; the main interest of the Indians was to secure the withdrawal of invaders from Kashmir as soon as possible.

Furthermore, Indians feel that their efforts at a positive contribution to the solution of the Kashmir dispute have not been correctly understood. Although the accession of the Maharaja of Jammu and Kashmir to India was a perfectly legal act in the Indian view, the Indian government nevertheless proposed on January 27, 1948, that an internationally supervised plebiscite on the matter be held in Kashmir, *provided* certain prior conditions were met. Because of the lapse of time since then and because of the misunderstandings which have overgrown the proposal, it deserves to be summarized here as essential to an understanding of the Indian point of view.

The first step suggested in the Indian draft proposal was that the fighting be ended. This was to be followed by the withdrawal of the invaders and by the return of all those who had fled during the raiding and subsequent fighting. Next, in order to restore normal political life, the emergency administration which had been appointed by the Maharaja during the days of chaos was to be changed into a responsible ministry and political prisoners were to be released. Then elections to a National Assembly were to be held on the basis of adult franchise, and a National (Kashmiri) government formed. Then and only then was the question of accession to be submitted to plebiscite by the National (Kashmiri) government "under the advice and observation of persons appointed by the United Nations." Both the prerequisites which India laid down and the character of the proposed international supervision have been obscured in subsequent discussions.

A positive reaction to this proposal was forthcoming only from the Chinese Nationalist representative on the Security Council; on March 18, 1948, he moved a resolution calling on Pakistan to desist from any further aid to the tribesmen and asking the interim Kashmir government to add representatives of Pakistan-occupied Azad Kashmir and to set up a plebiscite machinery to be directed by an appointee of the United Nations Secretary-General. India was disappointed to see that this proposal

did not receive more support from the other members of
the Council, who had by this time begun to feel that there
was more to the Kashmir case than was set forth in the
Indian complaint and that the Indians themselves were
not quite sure of their rights in the dispute.

To India it seemed that the situation was perverted by
the resolution sponsored by six powers including the
United States (but not the Soviet Union) and adopted on
April 21, 1948, which authorized the United Nations Commission set up in January to offer its good offices with respect both to "the restoration of peace and order and to
the holding of a plebiscite by the two governments. . . ."
By the "two governments" were meant the governments of
India *and* Pakistan. Indians have found it difficult to accept what they considered the cold-shouldering of their
complaint against the warlike acts of Pakistan; as the Indian delegate put it, the Security Council was "apologetic
to Pakistan for reminding it of its duty." Nor could Indian
opinion understand why the Council seized on the last of
India's draft proposals—plebiscite under United Nations
observation—and paid little attention to the other, prior
steps. The placing of Pakistan on an equal footing with
India as was done in the Council's decisions was also deeply
resented.

Within India these actions could not be regarded as impartial. To many Indians the American position appeared
to accept the Pakistan version of the Kashmir dispute and
to support Pakistan's claims to have a hand in Kashmiri
affairs. This conviction was strengthened when there was—
in the Indian view—not enough change in the Security
Council's attitude to Pakistan even after the United Nations Commission for India and Pakistan (UNCIP) had
learned in July 1948 that Pakistan troops had been fighting in Kashmir since the previous May. Furthermore, Indians have continued to feel that the United States has
favored Pakistan because at no time has the United States
brought any public pressure on Pakistan to withdraw its
troops unconditionally. (In rebuttal it is pointed out that

such unconditional withdrawal was not required by the relevant United Nations resolution.) Indian opinion was also disappointed because, although there has been considerable American criticism of India for resisting the decision of the United Nations, there has been no official American criticism of the continuing presence of Pakistan troops on what India has since October 26, 1947, come to consider Indian territory. This has seemed all the more surprising to Indians because the legality of Kashmir's accession to India has not been questioned by the United States or by the Security Council; in counterargument it is held that American acceptance of the accession has been framed in the context of a plebiscite to determine the final settlement of the Kashmir problem.

Indians believe that part of the difficulty arises from a tendency in the United States, as well as in other foreign countries, to draw a parallel between the struggle over Kashmir and the conflict over the accession of Junagadh in western India to Pakistan, while Indians are convinced that the two disputes arose from separate and distinct causes. In 1947 the Moslem Nawab of Junagadh signed an instrument of accession to Pakistan which was then nullified by action of the Diwan (Chief Minister); in turn the Diwan invited the government of India to restore law and order in Junagadh after violent demonstrations had broken out both among its predominantly Hindu population and also outside its borders, in India. A plebiscite in Junagadh under Indian auspices resulted in its accession to India. It is held in India that Americans and other foreigners make a misleading comparison between accession problems in Junagadh and in Kashmir when they argue that, while India participated in reversing the Moslem ruler's decision at the behest of a mainly Hindu population in Junagadh, it acted contrariwise in opposing Pakistan's efforts to reverse the accession decision of the Hindu Maharaja of Kashmir by calling for a plebiscite in that state with its majority of Moslems.

Indians hold it wrong to apply to disputes about the

accession of princely states the so-called two-nation theory
—that Hindus and Moslems constitute two nations. While
many Americans believe that this theory underlay the settlement of the independence question in the Indian subcontinent, Indians hold that they never accepted this theory
as valid but agreed to the partition of India as an unavoidable compromise. As regards the accession of princely states
in July 1947, Lord Mountbatten told the Chamber of
Princes that [1]

the States are theoretically free to link their future with which-
ever Dominion they may care. But when I say that they are at
liberty to link up with either of the Dominions, may I point
out that there are certain geographical compulsions which cannot be evaded.

The Indian government has maintained that, according
to the procedure accepted during the negotiations for independence by both the parties—the Congress party and
the Moslem League—the accession of Kashmir to India
was complete; it violated no legal, political or geographical
criterion that had been set up for the accession of princely
states. The contention that the Indian protest against
Junagadh's accession to Pakistan was based on the fact of
its Hindu population is not accepted by Indian opinion.
As far as Junagadh was concerned, India had protested because Junagadh territory was scattered over numerous en-
claves which were inextricably mixed up with the territories of numerous states which had already acceded to
India. If the administration of the scattered islands of
Junagadh territory had been vested in Pakistan it would
have created numerous, unending political and fiscal complications. It is generally believed in India that Pakistan's
primary interest in Junagadh was to secure a precedent
for questioning the validity of accession by the will of the
ruler—a precedent to apply in the case of Kashmir.

India also complains that despite what India regards as

[1] Earl Mountbatten of Burma, *Time Only to Look Forward:* Speeches
. . . as Viceroy of India . . . 1947–48 (London: Nicholas Kaye, 1949), p. 53.

its numerous concessions in the pursuit of the peaceful settlement of the Kashmir issue, both the Security Council
and the United States have continuously urged India to
proceed with plebiscite arrangements without having first
caused Pakistan to abide by the resolution of the UNCIP
of August 13, 1948.[2]

This resolution stated in Part II, A and B, that:

As the presence of troops of Pakistan in the territory of the
State of Jammu and Kashmir constitutes a material change in
the situation since it was represented by the Government of
Pakistan before the Security Council, the Government of Pakistan agrees to withdraw its troops from that State. . . .

When the Commission shall have notified the Government
of India that the tribesmen and Pakistan nationals referred to
in Part II, A2 hereof have withdrawn, thereby terminating the
situation which was represented by the Government of India
to the Security Council as having occasioned the presence of
Indian forces in the State of Jammu and Kashmir, and further,
that the Pakistan forces are being withdrawn from the State
of Jammu and Kashmir, the Government of India agrees to
begin to withdraw the bulk of their forces from that State in
stages to be agreed upon with the Commission.

During the discussions between the Commission and
Prime Minister Nehru regarding the plebiscite proposals
whose results were later incorporated in the resolution of
January 5, 1949, the latter had clearly indicated that, in
the event of Pakistan not accepting the proposals or, having accepted them, of its not implementing Parts I and II
of the resolution of August 13, 1948, "the Government of
India's acceptance of them should be regarded as in no
way binding upon them." This position, Indians point
out, had been accepted by Dr. Lozano (of Colombia) on
behalf of UNCIP. Indians complain that both the Security
Council and American opinion have increasingly tended
to ignore the essential point that the Indian offer was contingent upon the prior fulfillment of certain conditions

[2] For text of resolution, see UN, Security Council, 3rd year, *Documents*
(New York, 1948), S/995, pp. 3-5.

which have in fact not been fulfilled. India has felt itself under continuing pressure, to which it has not yielded, to change its stand on the validity of the Maharaja's accession and on the need for Pakistan's meeting the prior conditions set out by India before a plebiscite could be considered concretely.

Indians have often felt bitterly that Americans have ignored the cruelty and terror, arson and murder used by the tribal and other invaders in Kashmir with Pakistan's assent if not with its active help. They have complained that the United States, which was quick to move when Greece and other "cold war" areas were threatened and which was eager to condemn Communist China for its aggression in Korea, has in the Kashmir case consciously and even invidiously refrained from passing that judgment on Pakistan which alone would have cleared the invaders from Kashmir territory. They are of the opinion that despite the remarks of the United Nations mediator, Australian jurist Sir Owen Dixon, to the effect that the crossing by hostile elements of the Jammu and Kashmir frontier on October 20, 1947, and the movement of regular Pakistan forces into that state in May of 1948 were actions "contrary" to and "inconsistent" with international law,[3] the United States has been lending its support to the Pakistan charge that there had been Indian aggression in Kashmir for the purpose of securing Kashmir's accession by "fraud and violence." In the Indian view the United States should, instead, have supported the Indian charge of Pakistan aggression. All this feeling is directed as much at the Security Council as it is at the United States. In addition, American policy in the Kashmir dispute has been widely interpreted in India to be a reaction to India's refusal to align itself with the United States in the cold war. This trend in Indian thinking has become stronger since the 1954 American arms aid agreement with Pakistan.

There has also of late been an increasing awareness and

[3] UN, Security Council, 5th year, *Official Records, Supplement for September through December 1950* (New York, 1951), p. 29, para. 21.

fear in India of the unsettlement and upheavals that might be caused not only in Kashmir but also throughout Pakistan and India by the arousing of religious or communal passions that might accompany an attempt to refer the issue of accession to the Kashmiri people in the present situation. This apprehension has hardened the Indian view that the affairs of Kashmir should no longer be allowed to drift and that in the face of the Security Council's inability to clear Kashmir of the aggressor concrete steps had to be taken to order affairs in that part of Kashmir that was under Indian jurisdiction. From this conviction have followed the election of a constituent assembly in the Indian-occupied part of Kashmir, the drafting of a constitution and, in 1956 and 1957, the reaffirmation of Kashmir's integration with India, both in Indian and Kashmiri internal political arrangements and in the Indian position as presented to the Security Council.

In the United States the essential points at issue in the Kashmir case have generally been appraised quite differently. American opinion has come to recognize the great strategic and psychological value of Kashmir to India and to Pakistan, as well as its potential economic importance to both. Kashmir's northern frontier, which lies close to the Soviet Union and borders on China, has importance as marking the upper limit of the Indian-Pakistan subcontinent. Kashmir's position on the flank of both Indian and Pakistan territories means that possession by either country must complicate the other's defense problems. Its snows fill the four major rivers that irrigate West Pakistan and parts of Indian Punjab. Furthermore its population—about three-quarters Moslem, out of a total of some four millions —is of extreme interest to both countries, as in both countries its ultimate allegiance involves deeply held tenets. Pakistan identifies the Kashmiris with its separate Islamic statehood; India, whose population includes some forty million Moslems—who in no other region of India constitute a majority—identifies the Kashmiris with its demonstration of a secular statehood that attempts to establish equal rights for followers of all religions. Because the national prestige and purposes of India and Pakistan are equally and fully committed to the possession of Kashmir, the dangers inherent in the dispute are great. They have come to be fully recognized in the United States.

The widely held American view that the Kashmir dispute could not be settled by a straightforward acceptance of India's original complaint evolved from several considerations. There was first of all the widespread reaction of shock to the communal outbreaks that spread across West Pakistan and upper India after August 1947. There was a feeling that there was little to choose between Moslem excesses on the one hand and Hindu and Sikh excesses on the other; stories of how the minorities were driven out of such places as Bahawalpur and Kapurthala showed how deeply the princely states were also involved. Although the popular frenzy had somewhat spent itself by January 1948, the tone of the submissions to the Security Council in that month, the Junagadh situation and the virtual "civil war" in Kashmir that followed on the Maharaja's bloody repression in Poonch, all these suggested that Pakistan and India were still at each other's throats. The assassination by a Hindu of Mahatma Gandhi at the end of that same month destroyed for many Americans what belief may have remained that the responsibility for the unfortunate developments of 1947 lay wholly on Pakistan's side. Thus the violence in Kashmir seemed to be part of a larger pattern of violence. This suggested to Americans as well as others that India, the complainant, had not come before the Security Council with "clean hands" but that both countries had become ensnared in tragic developments. The prevailing American reaction, therefore, was that it would be unrealistic to try to solve the Kashmir dispute by adjudication of the legal points—namely, the validity of the Maharaja's accession to India and the allegation of Pakistan aggression—that were advanced by India but denied by Pakistan.

Fortunately, as it appeared in American eyes, there was

one feature common to the Indian and Pakistan approaches, a feature that might well serve as a basis for progress toward a solution: the plebiscite proposal. In its original submission to the Security Council [4] the Indian government had given an assurance that,

once the soil of the State had been cleared of the invader and normal conditions restored, its people would be free to decide their future by the recognized democratic method of a plebiscite or referendum, which, in order to ensure complete impartiality, might be held under international auspices.

Pakistan, too, stood for an internationally supervised plebiscite in Kashmir. Since India and Pakistan could not agree on the origin or indeed the nature of the dispute, the United States felt that it was not necessary to go back to arguing over earlier causes and held that the best chance of solving the dispute lay in achieving agreement on the conditions of the plebiscite. This view was strengthened when both India and Pakistan, in the light of the clarifications given to them respectively, accepted the resolutions passed by UNCIP on August 13, 1948, and January 5, 1949, setting out conditions for a cease-fire, truce and plebiscite and reiterating that "the question of the accession of the State of Jammu and Kashmir to India or Pakistan will be decided through the democratic method of a free and impartial plebiscite."

It has since been held in the United States that when India (and Pakistan) accepted these two resolutions the question of Pakistan's aggression or of the validity of the Maharaja's accession became outdated inasmuch as the plebiscite itself was to determine the future disposition of the state. American support for the Commission's work was later extended to the mediatory efforts of General A. G. L. McNaughton, Sir Owen Dixon and Dr. Frank Graham, then to bilateral negotiations between India and Pakistan, and in February 1957 to the mission of Mr.

4 UN, Security Council, 3rd year, *Documents*, cited, S/628, p. 3.

Gunnar Jarring of Sweden, President of the Security Council at the time.

In the course of the protracted negotiations from 1948 onwards, the impression gained currency in the United States that India more than Pakistan was resisting proposals for demilitarization and for plebiscite conditions that seemed reasonable to impartial outsiders. The essence of a free and fair plebiscite is that the voters should not be intimidated or the result unfairly affected either by opponents of the existing regime or by the government of the day. Experience in other plebiscites held elsewhere under international auspices has shown that these conditions can be obtained only through enforcement of an almost complete, if temporary, demilitarization and through full control over the plebiscite machinery by an agency having the power to function entirely independently of the existing government of the region. Whereas Pakistan, for whatever reasons, has accepted measures that appear to ensure these conditions, Indian responses to the succession of United Nations negotiators have implied, in American eyes, an unwillingness to agree to the temporary concessions of sovereignty and military control necessary for the conduct of an impartial plebiscite. This very point was emphasized by Sir Owen Dixon, in reporting the failure of his mediatory effort. "In the end," he said,[5]

I became convinced that India's agreement would never be obtained to demilitarization in any such form, or to provisions governing the period of the plebiscite of any such character, as would in my opinion permit of the plebiscite being conducted in conditions sufficiently guarding against intimidation and other forms of influence and abuse by which the freedom and fairness of the plebiscite might be imperilled.

Another facet of India's policy that has been regretted in the United States lies in its later interpretations of the resolutions to which it had agreed in 1948 and 1949. In the intricate negotiations to find a way of implementing

[5] UN, Security Council, 5th year, *Official Records, Supplement* . . ., cited, p. 36, para. 52.

these resolutions, United Nations negotiators repeatedly took the position that all the steps of truce and plebiscite were interrelated and that neither party was likely to agree to take the first step unless it had full assurance that the remaining steps would follow automatically. India's insistence at various stages that Pakistan carry out the first step, that of withdrawing its troops from territory under its *de facto* control, before agreeing on the detailed arrangements for conducting a plebiscite, has seemed to Americans to smack of a debater's point, one intended to delay rather than to facilitate a settlement.

It has seemed to many in the United States that a plebiscite could have been organized at any time and carried out within a very few months and that its result would have made purely academic all the other issues on which India has stood fast in its resistance to United Nations proposals. Demilitarization would be a temporary matter, to last at most one summer season; hardly long enough, Americans have believed, to justify the protracted arguments over the stages and extent of demilitarization that have stopped all progress toward a plebiscite. Similarly the problem of assigning jurisdiction over different parts of Kashmir during the plebiscite period has seemed to Americans to have been exaggerated beyond its inherent significance, especially in view of the agreement that the plebiscite would be conducted under wholly impartial auspices.

Again, many Americans, recalling India's pledge in 1951, when a constituent assembly was set up in Kashmir, that that Assembly's actions would not be binding upon India in violation of India's international commitments, have been disappointed that by 1957 India had accepted the Kashmir Assembly's reaffirmation of the state's accession to India and had apparently rejected any further consideration of a plebiscite. By taking such a position India has in effect seemed to be going back on the formal agreement it reached with Pakistan and the United Nations in 1948 and 1949.

In the continuing absence of agreement between India and Pakistan, American opinion came to hold that the parties had some obligation to heed the resolutions of the Security Council to which they had themselves assented. The impression gained currency that, whereas Pakistan pressed mostly for stronger action by the Security Council, India maintained the position that the Security Council could take no step in Kashmir without its consent. It seems to Americans that this position is a far cry from the active efforts which India has made to move the United Nations to strong action against some other countries, including South Africa, Israel, France and Britain, despite the opposition of those countries. Furthermore, it has become a general American view that, after taking the Kashmir complaint to the United Nations, India has reacted to Security Council resolutions in a unilateral fashion that has not only damaged India's prestige but has undermined the influence of the United Nations.

Americans have been particularly disturbed by the assertions of leading spokesmen of the Indian government that positions taken in the Kashmir case by the United States and by the Security Council, when they were adverse to the Indian position, were the result of hostility toward India and of conspiracy or collusion with Pakistan rather than the result of honest differences with India's policies. While realizing that Indian emotions are aroused to high pitch over Kashmir, many Americans have been disturbed that American efforts to encourage a conciliatory settlement should be regarded in India as suspect. If it were a question of the United States exerting pressure on India to adopt a course of action to which it had never agreed, the matter would be different; but in the prevailing American view the main outlines of the Kashmir case were set by the agreement between India and Pakistan in the two UNCIP resolutions that the disposition of Kashmir would be decided by a plebiscite.

For these several reasons, much American opinion has been critical of India's conduct in the Kashmir case. As

Americans see it, there is no question of the United States favoring one party or the other, but only the question of each party's willingness to carry out basic agreements and to follow recognized international standards in resolving a dispute which they had brought to the attention of the United Nations. It is on this point that American sympathy toward India has been most strained.

At the same time there is some minority opinion in the United States which supports the Indian argument that a plebiscite as a means of resolving the Kashmir dispute has been outdated by the march of events in recent years. To start with, this opinion would agree with the statement to the Security Council by Gunnar Jarring in April of 1957 that [6]

. . . the implementation of international agreements of an *ad hoc* character, which has not been achieved fairly speedily, may become progressively more difficult because the situation with which they were to cope has tended to change.

There are also other reasons in support of this view, reasons which may be listed as follows: the Kashmir government has brought into effect many measures improving the lot of the people and it would be a step backward to call into question the authority of that government; strong social tensions might be created by the process of holding a plebiscite—perhaps strong enough to put into jeopardy the security and lives of thousands or even millions of people in the State of Jammu and Kashmir itself and perhaps in India and Pakistan. Those who hold this view argue that plebiscite electioneering would inevitably emphasize the religious loyalties of Moslems and presumably their identification on religious grounds with the Islamic Republic of Pakistan. Should Kashmir go to Pakistan as a result of a plebiscite, there are those who fear that the Hindus of Kashmir would find living conditions intolerable and would flee to India, thereby reinfecting pub-

[6] UN, Security Council, *Report on the India-Pakistan Question Submitted in Pursuance of the Resolution of the Security Council of 21 February 1957 (S/3793)*, S/3821 (New York, April 29, 1957), p. 6.

lic life with the virus of communalism. This might destroy the peaceful position that the minority community of forty million Moslems has attained in India as well as react adversely on the status of the Hindus still living in East Pakistan and even revive the horrors of the mass migration of 1947. While the government of India presumably has a far better grip on law and order now than it had during the large-scale disturbances of the partition years, the danger of renewed communal troubles under such circumstances is definitely not ruled out by Indian officials.

If there are serious objections to the holding of a plebiscite so long after the Kashmir dispute began, the question whether any alternative mode of settlement can be found remains. Any course on which India and Pakistan could agree would probably be regarded with favor by the United States. On this basis, suggestions for holding a plebiscite in the Valley of Kashmir alone, coupled with the partitioning of the remaining areas, have at times caught American attention as possible solutions. Such suggestions are, however, still far removed from the official Indian view that with the outmoding of the plebiscite agreement the only course for the United Nations is to find Pakistan guilty of aggression and to clear Pakistan forces from the soil of Kashmir.

American Arms Aid to Pakistan

The prospects of adjustments in India's policies that might open the way to a wider area of agreement between India and the United States on the solution of the Kashmir issue appear to have been adversely affected by the new factor of American arms aid to Pakistan, which was begun in 1954. This development needs examination here because, although there was no intention to do so in the United States, this step very decisively affected Indian attitudes toward the Kashmir dispute and toward the United States. It might be pointed out however that while American arms aid to Pakistan was not emphasized by the Indian delegate in the Security Council debates on Kashmir of January-February 1957, it seemed as though the subject had been brought up in the discussions Mr. Jarring had with Indian government leaders in New Delhi. In his Report to the Security Council, Mr. Jarring said that he [7]

. . . could not fail to take note of the concern expressed in connection with the changing political, economic and strategic factors surrounding the whole of the Kashmir question, together with the changing pattern of power relations in West and South Asia.

In November 1953 rumors began to be heard that the United States was considering a request from Pakistan for military aid. Prime Minister Nehru referred to the matter in a press conference on November 15 and next day the Indian Ambassador called on the Secretary of State to seek information about the proposed pact. On February 24, 1954, President Eisenhower announced that the United States, "gravely concerned over the weakness of defensive capabilities in the Middle East," was complying with a request by Pakistan for military aid. That the President appeared to be informed that this action might lead to an adverse reaction in India was well reflected in his announcement.[8] "Let me make it clear," he said,

that we shall be guided by the stated purposes and requirements of the mutual security legislation. Those include specifically the provision that equipment, materials or services provided will be used solely to maintain the recipient country's internal security and for its legitimate self-defense, or to permit it to participate in the defense of the area of which it is a part. Any recipient country also must undertake that it will not engage in any act of aggression against any other nation.

These undertakings afford adequate assurance to all nations, regardless of their political orientation and whatever their international policies may be, that the arms the United States provides for the defense of the free world will in no way threaten their own security. I can say that if our aid to any country, in-

[7] Same.
[8] *Department of State Bulletin,* v. 30 (March 15, 1954), p. 401.

cluding Pakistan, is misused and directed against another in aggression I will undertake immediately, in accordance with my constitutional authority, appropriate action both within and without the United Nations to thwart such aggression. I would also consult with the Congress on further steps.

In a personal letter President Eisenhower assured Prime Minister Nehru that the action "is not directed in any way against India," that he was recommending to Congress the continuation of American economic and technical aid to India, and that "if your Government should conclude that circumstances require military aid of a type contemplated by our mutual security legislation, please be assured that your request would receive my most sympathetic consideration."

The President had not been misinformed about probable Indian reactions. Prime Minister Nehru dismissed the American offer of military aid as gratuitous, since it was public knowledge that India would not accept military assistance from any foreign power. The Prime Minister declared that the provision of American military aid to Pakistan had destroyed the "roots and foundations" of the proposed plebiscite in Kashmir and had completely altered the political and military character of the dispute. Indians feared that the effect of the military aid program would be to make Pakistan more intractable. It could now count on United States support in case of trouble and its capacity to intimidate the Kashmiris or to launch an attack on India would be increased. The conclusion was widely accepted in India that the United States had ceased to be neutral in the Kashmir issue since it was now an ally of Pakistan. Prime Minister Nehru charged that India was being encircled by Pakistan's military arrangements and that large bases had been built not only in Pakistan "but so far as my knowledge goes, military bases have been set up in Pakistan-occupied territories of Kashmir."

The Prime Minister's views were developed and expanded in the Indian press and on political platforms to the point that the United States came to be regarded in many quarters as the principal cause of India's insecurity in its relations with Pakistan and of Pakistan's intransigence. True, Nehru and other opinion leaders stated later that they did not believe that it had been the United States' intention, in giving military aid to Pakistan, to cause trouble for India, but that Pakistan's motives in requesting aid, as indicated in many public statements by Pakistan leaders, were quite different from those of the United States.

The extension of the military pact system beyond the Latin American and the North Atlantic Treaty areas, where Americans had generally approved this new approach to regional security, to additional parts of the world gave rise to much debate in the United States. While the Pakistan pact was being negotiated, there was at first considerable opposition within the United States to this and other departures from a traditional American foreign policy. However, since then the opposition has died down and Congressional and general opinion has apparently come to accept the military assistance programs of the present.

The reasons brought out in favor of the Pakistan agreement were many. For some time Pakistan had thrown out feelers on the question of entering into a defensive alliance with the United States, together with Turkey and other countries that believed the formation of a common front against the danger of Soviet aggression was the best way to prevent that danger from becoming a reality. While the "northern tier" grouping might not in itself constitute an effective military bulwark against Soviet attack, it seemed likely to reduce the danger of "little wars" breaking out along the periphery of the Communist bloc. Assisting Pakistan to improve the equipment, mobility, training and organization of its force would, it was thought, render less rather than more likely a Soviet attempt to overrun or subvert the country. Finally it should be recalled that military aid was only a part of the assistance that the United States offered Pakistan, a large volume of economic aid also being pledged to it on the ground that the healthy development of Pakistan was the best insurance of its peace and stability against any internal or external threats.

In general terms, it was the American view that the interests of the free world would best be served by actions strengthening both India and Pakistan and that these ends could best be accomplished if both countries moved forward in peace toward stability and economic development. It was also an American assumption that military aid to Pakistan would constitute no threat to Indian security. This assessment was based partly on the relative size and strength of India and Pakistan, with India having nearly four times the area of Pakistan, four times the population, probably ten times the industrial base, and superior strength in most other measurable dimensions. It was also based on the assurances of the Pakistan government that the military aid would be used for the designated common purposes of defense against Soviet attack. Presumably American authorities assumed that even if Pakistan, despite its relative weakness and its official pledges, were to determine on a seemingly hopeless aggression against India, American influence would be adequate to forestall the action or, at the worst, to bring it to a prompt end. Americans have felt that India could have placed more confidence in American assurances.

The Indian position differs at almost every point. The extension of the military pact system to Asia continues to be criticized. It is believed in India that the acceptance of American military aid has been made palatable to public opinion not because there is any real danger but because it was represented as being advantageous in local rivalries; this has tended to harden instead of to soothe local conflicts. In the case of Pakistan, this general position is reinforced by the estimate in India of Pakistan's policies and of political, economic and social conditions in that country. Statements by Nehru and others underscore the Indian fear that Pakistan is a politically unstable entity, that to hold public support its leaders consciously stir up irritants between India and itself, and that Pakistan is making conditions increasingly intolerable for its Hindu citizens. They believe that, if their power to govern should be critically weakened, the leaders of Pakistan would seek to restore their domestic authority by launching a disguised aggression against India or even by a stab at Srinagar, the capital of Kashmir. Such a chain of reactions, in the Indian view, could not be broken by United States influence in time to avert disaster.

Indian resentment of American arms aid to Pakistan can be explained in large part by the fact that by allying itself with the United States Pakistan has "aligned" itself with one side in the cold war. This runs counter to basic Indian concepts of foreign policy. To the Indian way of thinking such alignment endangers India's security by bringing the clashing interests of the major powers to the borders of India. By joining the Baghdad Pact and SEATO Pakistan has also presumably sought to strengthen its own general influence in international affairs, an influence which India suspects. By this alignment Pakistan has also taken a position different from that of India in Western Asia, where India feels that its security and other interests are best served by encouraging "neutralism," by cultivating extremely friendly relations with Egypt, and by befriending the Arab countries and cold-shouldering Israeli claims.

Another factor that helps explain the Indian reaction is that to Indians the great disparity between Indian and Pakistan strength is no guarantee against Pakistan aggression. They recall that Pakistan sent its troops into Kashmir in 1948, at a time when it was still very weak, to fight against the Indian army. Indians are persuaded that Pakistan has asked for American arms aid primarily for use against India rather than against the Soviet Union or China. That its use would not necessarily be solely defensive is accepted in India because of repeated references by Pakistan speakers to a "holy war" to liberate Kashmir from India. Barring attack, Indians feel that Pakistan is interested in American arms in order to improve its bargaining position against India.

Because of the impact of fears, attachments and historical experience on the Indian outlook, it is doubtful that Indian resentment of American arms aid to Pakistan will be moderated while tensions continue high between India and Pakistan. In these circumstances a very narrow basis exists for reducing the tensions between India and the United States on the aid question. Yet some steps seem to be possible.

First of all, it would be helpful if the nature of the American aid program could be better understood in India, especially the relative roles of "economic" and "military" aid. Apparently it is not yet accepted in India that these are to some extent artificial and budgetary categories; even major allocations grouped under "military" aid often support the general economy directly. Apart from these "defense support" funds, substantial help also goes into construction activities which serve equally the demands of national defense and of national welfare, for example, through building new roads or setting up new factories for the production of prepared foods, clothing and other personal supplies, household equipment, machines and the like. A considerable portion of American military aid to Pakistan is devoted to strengthening the economy in these and similar ways, in addition to supplying its armed forces with modern military weapons. It might also be argued that any "economic" aid to a country that does not receive "military" aid is in a sense "defense support," as it makes possible a larger defense budget appropriation from domestic funds.

A second helpful step would be to allay the fears of the Indian government that American military aid will make the Pakistan military establishment stronger than India's or at least strengthen it significantly in relation to the Indian military establishment. Since the details of military establishments are naturally shrouded in great secrecy, it is impossible for unofficial persons to determine whether the fire power, mobility, etc. of military equipment that Pakistan is receiving under the aid agreement is less, as much or more than that of military equipment which India purchases from abroad. In view of the lack of any authoritative information, Indians' worst fears are aroused. And among the people there is a widely held belief that with American aid Pakistan will achieve parity or near parity with India in a short time. A number of informed Americans believe, however, that because Pakistan is markedly weaker and smaller, and also geographically divided, its economy, even with foreign aid, could hardly sustain a growth in the military establishment which would come near to closing the gap between the Indian and Pakistan armed forces. Other possible ameliorative measures might be found in giving strengthened assurances that Pakistan will not use American-donated arms to attack India and in an increased emphasis on American economic rather than military aid to Pakistan. But these would be only ameliorative; so long as Indians fear Pakistan, American military aid to Pakistan is certain to disturb friendly Indian-American relations.

In both the Kashmir issue and the arms aid question the causes of the Indian-American tension are in the realities of Indian-Pakistan relations. So long as they are as severely strained as they have been since 1947, Indian opinion is certain to resent any support given by the United States to proposals in the Kashmir issue that are favored by Pakistan, or any American contribution to the strengthening of Pakistan's military forces. It is hardly necessary to point out that under present conditions American support to Indian positions is likely to be similarly resented in Pakistan. And when India suggests that because of its difficulties with Pakistan the United States should not proceed with Pakistan to strengthen their joint plans against the danger of Soviet aggression, Americans are apt to be resentful too.

This brief review has suggested how strongly India's approach to Pakistan is dominated by security interests, in contrast to India's policies toward most other countries. Because India views Pakistan as an immediate and continuing threat to its security, its policies toward its neighbor have been very similar to policies which have commonly been adopted by the larger military powers under similar feelings of danger. The United States can respect India for taking protective measures. There is, however, a feeling in the United States that India, which has taken a leading role in urging other countries along peaceful paths, has not helped the general problem of resolving international tensions by its policy toward Pakistan. Similarly, many Indians ask why the United States should criticize Indian policy toward Pakistan when it is in Indian eyes parallel to the American policy toward the Soviet Union. As we have seen, difficulties in communication between India and the United States on the Pakistan question run deep. There exists almost a stereotype in India of an America that is helping Pakistan out of a sense of hostility to India. This is matched by the belief sometimes found in the United States that India prefers a weak Pakistan on its borders out of a desire to ensure its own superior position in the region.

The real hope for improved Indian-American adjustments in the field of their relations with Pakistan arises from the prospect that India and Pakistan can gradually or perhaps at a stroke resolve their troubles. After all, the disputes over Kashmir and arms aid are two among a great many difficulties between India and Pakistan, of which a number have already been resolved by compromise and negotiation while still more are under peaceful discussion between the two countries. Representatives of India and Pakistan have frequently expressed their hopes for improved mutual relations, and this must also be the hope of those who are concerned over the difficulties that Pakistan questions inject into Indian-American relations.

Chapter 5

EAST AND SOUTHEAST ASIA

EXCEPTING Soviet Asia and Thailand, every country from the Pacific Ocean to the Khyber Pass has since 1945 undergone drastic political transformation as part of the new consciousness of national dignity and social aspiration that has swept across Asia. In some cases this transformation has been diverted into the paths of communism, in others it has moved with varying success into more democratic patterns. Korea, freed from Japanese domination, partitioned, and then plunged into a new war, has since the cease-fire in 1953 been seeking to combine independence with economic viability—at least in the south. Japan, defeated, then occupied until 1951, is now working out a new status under a parliamentary democracy. Independence movements have achieved their political goals in ten former dependencies of Western powers: in the Philippines in 1946, India and Pakistan in 1947, Burma and Ceylon in 1948, Indonesia in 1949, Laos, Cambodia and Viet Nam in 1954 and Malaya in 1957. Singapore has gained large installments of promised self-rule. In Nepal, the Rana-controlled oligarchy with India's encouragement yielded authority to a monarchy that is seeking to build up parliamentary institutions. And in China, the long-drawn-out civil war which resulted in the flight of the Nationalist government to Formosa, placed the Chinese Communist party in control of the mainland with ambitions to create— for the first time in modern history—a major Asian power along the northern land frontiers of India and Southeast Asia.

Inevitably all these changes—which encompassed India and transformed the character of American concern with Asia—have also had their influence on Indian-American relations. Not all the changes have struck the two peoples with equal force. India, for example, has laid more constant stress on the need for ending colonialism everywhere than has the United States, though both have favored the trend and—if we may anticipate the subject matter of another chapter—it seems unlikely that they will be seriously divided in the future over colonial issues in Southeast Asia. Similarly, Japan, which holds a central place in American interests, has been rather distant from India emotionally as well as geographically, as are Korea, the Republic of the Philippines and even Thailand. India has some contacts with each of them but they do not figure prominently in Indian-American relations. Indeed, Pakistan apart, there are very few Indian-American differences on Asian questions except those that in one way or another reflect the advent of Communist governments in China, North Korea and North Viet Nam, or the possibility of further Communist penetration into Asia.

At the heart of Indian-American differences over East Asia is the so-called "China Question," which the two countries approach from profoundly divergent perspectives. These differences may directly involve their policies toward the two Chinese governments—as they have in the matters of the recognition of Communist China and its representation in the United Nations or in the matter of the disposition of Korea. Or they may be a degree removed and involve the interaction of Indian and American policies toward Chinese Communist moves in other countries, as for example Communist penetration into Tibet or Chinese policies toward Southeast Asia and Korea. In these matters the clash between India and the United States may not be direct but it is not for that reason in the long run less serious as basic attitudes and concerns are also involved.

The "China Question": to the End of the Civil War

It is doubtful whether India and the United States would have differed over China if Chiang Kai-shek had won the civil war in 1949 and retained control over his country. The leaders of Indian nationalism as well as the American people and government had a number of ties with China and friendly, admiring relations with Chiang, who had long been viewed in both countries as an outstanding nationalist leader.

Actually, modern Indian interest in China may be dated from the Chinese revolution of 1911–1912. The sympathy of many Indians with Sun Yat-sen's efforts in turn stimulated a revival of interest in India's quite remarkable contacts with ancient China which—stretching from the first to the eleventh centuries—had included considerable travel and trade, and had seen the spread of Buddhism from India to China. Spurred on thus by political sympathies and historical memories, Indian nationalist leaders set about renewing contacts between the two countries in modern times. Such events as Rabindranath Tagore's visit to the Far East in 1924 and Jawaharlal Nehru's first contacts with Chinese political figures excited great public interest. Two presidents of the Congress party during the 1920's suggested, for example, establishing an "Asiatic Federation," to consist of the peoples of India, China and Southeast Asia.

This interest grew in the 1930's. Indian opinion like American opinion was outraged by the Japanese aggression against China in 1931 and 1937. Indian newspapers called on the League of Nations to apply military sanctions against Japan. The Congress party passed resolutions and organized demonstrations on "China Days." In response to an international appeal for help by the commander of the Communist-led Chinese Eighth Route Army, a privately-supported Indian ambulance unit was sent to China. In 1939 Nehru visited China and in early 1942 he brought Chiang in touch with other Indian nationalists when the Chinese leader came to India to appeal for more support against the Japanese at that critical stage. Although Chiang failed to persuade the Congress party leaders to support the Allied war effort, Nehru described his visit as "a great event in India" as a result of which "the bonds that tied India and China grew stronger." Other prominent figures also eulogized Chiang and China's resistance to aggression.

American contacts with China—while of more recent origin than India's—were for long of a more concentrated and intense nature. By World War II the United States had come to know China through a century's intercourse at missionary, trading and political levels. No other Asian nation had attracted so much American interest. American private citizens had given large-scale support to educational and medical centers in China. On the political level, the United States had since the first Chinese-American Treaty of 1844 in various ways sought to limit the encroachments of foreign powers on China and to resist the whittling down of Chinese sovereignty by Russia, West European states and Japan. Thus in pursuing its own economic and political aims of preserving a united and independent China, the United States had sought to serve also the interests of the weak Chinese government. This interest in China continued and in the 1930's the Japanese invasion of China provoked great indignation in the United States, as it did in India. The American government refused to recognize the Manchukuo regime set up by the Japanese. When the United States and China became allies during World War II, their contacts increased in range and intimacy and substantial American help for several years supported Chiang's efforts to meet his most pressing military and domestic problems.

The postwar period, which brought independence to India, brought disaster to the Nationalist government in China. At first it appeared probable that Chiang would reestablish the authority of his government in the territories that had been occupied by Japan and in those which the Chinese Communists had made their base for some ten years. Expectations that China would at last play an effective part in world affairs were reflected in American insistence that China receive a permanent seat on the United Nations Security Council. A similar expectation was also involved in the strengthening of India's diplomatic relations with China shortly after Nehru came to power, and in the Prime Minister's welcoming the Nationalist Chinese representatives to the unofficial Asian Relations Conference in 1947.

But the great social, economic and political ravages of the Japanese occupation—which had continued for fourteen years in Manchuria and eight years in China proper—with the attendant stresses of civil war had undermined the foundations of the Kuomintang government. The dismantling of America's great military power—begun as soon as the war ended—left Chiang facing his domestic and foreign problems virtually alone. His handling of them elicited criticism at home and abroad. Though distressed at signs of disintegration in China, Americans stood aside and pressed Chiang to seek a compromise settlement with his Communist rivals. The Chinese Communists, however, strengthened by the Japanese military stores left them by the Russian military regime in Manchuria at the end of World War II and by American equipment captured from dispirited troops in Chiang's command, and helped by widespread dissatisfaction with the Kuomintang regime, swept southward through province after province.

By this time Americans were engaged in a bitter controversy as to whether the United States could have prevented this debacle. A sense of having failed in its mission in China spread through the United States, along with an awareness that Communist victory in China would heighten the threat posed by the Soviet Union. Indian government and public opinion, by contrast, took the climactic developments calmly. Enthusiasm for Chiang had long since evaporated on the ground that he had failed to achieve administrative and social reforms and was un-duly dependent on American support. With the ending of civil war and the establishment of a strong regime, many Indians saw China at last coming into its own after a long period of humiliation and foreign intervention. On De-cember 30, 1949, the Indian government recognized the newly proclaimed Central People's Government of the Peo-ple's Republic of China, whereas the United States re-jected the Communists' claims to sovereignty over China at it had the Japanese claims in the 1930's.

Responses to the Communist Victory

Americans' first direct experiences with the Chinese Communist regime hardened their attitude. American dip-lomats who had stayed at their posts in China during the civil war were treated harshly by the new authorities and in violation of accepted international practice. The Com-munist government's seizure and imprisonment of Amer-ican nationals aroused bitter resentment. These actions, and the Sino-Soviet treaty of alliance, signed in February 1950, which confirmed the close links between Soviet Rus-sia and the Chinese Communist government, were har-bingers of other developments that soon followed. The Communist aggression against South Korea and China's role in prolonging the war kept American opinion strongly antagonistic to the Chinese Communist regime. At the same time there were and continue to be lively discussions in the United States over the policy it should adopt toward Communist China.

In India also various considerations have been involved in policy toward mainland China. On the one hand India from the beginning took the position that, as the Commu-nist regime had in fact come out uppermost in the civil war and as revolutionary changes were taking place in China, other nations could help make and keep the transi-tion a peaceful one by showing understanding and sym-

pathy for the new regime. Many Indians reasoned that unless the new Chinese regime were generally accepted, its
leaders would become embittered and isolated from the
main currents of world affairs as well as unduly dependent
on the Soviet Union. Since—in spite of their both being
Asian nations—India and China have nevertheless been far
removed from each other, the Indian government set out
soon after recognition to enlarge Sino-Indian contacts
through the exchange of students, of cultural and trade
missions and through diplomatic measures.

At the same time however there is a frequent recognition within India that China is in fact its most potent
Asian rival. Thus—while Indians take pride in the ability
of an Asian people to face up successfully to hitherto
stronger Western powers—there is also a sense that the
Chinese are competing with India for influence over the
future of Asia. The Indian government is aware of the
forced-draft methods of the Chinese Communists and it
understands the crucial nature of the competition between
these methods and those of India for the allegiance of
Southeast Asia and other underdeveloped areas. It is also
possible to surmise that the *Pancha Shil* policy developed
by Nehru in 1954 and discussed below represents an effort to secure the commitment of the Chinese Communist
government publicly to certain principles of state action
in the hope that this will allay the fears of the small states
bordering China without at the same time involving the
Indian government in an expensive policy of opposition
to possible Chinese moves—a policy which India feels it
need not pursue at present.

In spite of this awareness in India and the rejection by
many thoughtful Indians of Chinese Communist domestic
methods, there is a significant difference in Indian and
American reactions toward developments within China.
Generally speaking, as we have already pointed out, Indians do not share the moral repugnance toward communism that most Americans feel. They believe that the Chinese people had a right to choose whatever form of gov-

ernment they desired and that it was no concern of outsiders what that choice was. Most Americans feel that
no real choice was made by the Chinese people. They also
feel that the internal character of a Communist government permeates the actions that it takes toward other nations and in turn must influence the assumptions on which
other nations base their policies toward a Communist
state.

It has been a matter of more intense concern in the
United States than in India that the new Chinese system
differs in its fundamentals from the patterns of government acceptable in democratically oriented nations that
share basic elements of a democratic tradition. In spite of
various camouflaging devices, all power in mainland China
rests in the hands of the top party leadership which has at
its command propaganda instruments, a secret police, large
armies and a highly organized system of party cells backed
by an elaborate system of inspection that reaches down to
the lowest levels. In such a system the individual is regarded merely as an instrument to serve the interests of
the dictatorial party. Thus the new regime is trying to
reduce or eliminate the traditional system of family inter-
dependence and to replace it by the direct loyalty of each
individual to the party and the state. In the American view
the system of totalitarian control has also eliminated regional and other loyalties to an unusual degree and given
the party state a remarkable degree of control over the
lives, activities and patterns of thought of the people.

The Communist party is also engaged in an ambitious
program of reconstruction and industrialization. The regime has undertaken to reorganize agriculture along cooperative and collective lines and claims that some ninety
per cent of the peasants have already been "collectivized"
under varying degrees of control by the party and the state.
Substantial unrest reported by the party press in various
provinces has been dealt with severely and the large flood
control and other construction jobs are heavily manned
by "corrective" labor. Many Indians seem to have re-

ceived satisfaction from the attempts of the new government to build up China's economy and power. It is a serious question in the minds of most Americans, but few if
any Indians, whether the economic gains will bring benefit
to the masses of the Chinese people or will simply increase
the ability of the regime to strengthen its control within
the country and take over gradually, from the Soviet
sources of supply, the problem of equipping the very large
military forces which are being maintained by the Chinese
Communist leaders. China, with the Soviet government
supplying the more elaborate military equipment, has become one of the five major military powers of the world.

Impressions vary as to how heavy the cost has been in
human terms. There are different opinions as to how many
persons have been killed by the regime, how many sent to
"corrective labor," how many to "indoctrination centers." It seems possible to say that many people in India
and certainly most Americans are convinced that under
Chinese Communist rule, as under Soviet rule, the individual has no human rights as the term is understood in democracies based on Western traditions. Prime Minister
Nehru himself has said that Chinese methods are not for
India. There remains however a lively interest in India in
Chinese progress and voices are heard querying whether
some of the Chinese methods—of labor allocation or land
reform for example—might not be useful in India and
whether in order to keep China from forging ahead of it,
India might not perhaps adopt some of them.

Differences in evaluation of the Chinese Communist domestic order serve as an irritant in Indian-American relations, as do differences in evaluation of the Soviet system.
However, the more acute issues concern rather the impact
of Chinese policies on world affairs and the most suitable
international postures to adopt toward Communist China.
In Indian-American terms, the major issues have been the
recognition of Communist China and its seating in the
United Nations, and the future of Formosa. In India, opinion seems firm on these matters. In the United States dis-

cussion of these issues continues, with a degree of change in at least some aspects of American policy toward Communist China not to be completely ruled out.

Recognition and Seating in the United Nations

The recognition of one regime as the government of China and the seating of a regime in the United Nations as the accredited representative of China are separate issues, but they are closely interrelated, leaning as they do on the same arguments and bringing into play the same emotions.

Both issues rest on a combination of formal arguments and political considerations. In the absence of uniformly accepted criteria of legitimacy, India has in most though not all cases followed the simple doctrine that *de facto* control of territory and administration entitles a government to *de jure* status. India—the second non-Communist government to extend recognition to the Communist government of China—did so on this basis. The United States has since the time of Jefferson, in most but not all periods of its history, applied three criteria for recognition: control over the machinery of state; government with the assent of the people or at least without their open opposition; and the willingness and ability of a regime to fulfill its international obligations. Failure to meet the second and third standards, or either of them, has in the twentieth century delayed or prevented American recognition of several Latin American regimes, of the Soviet Union, Manchukuo, and the Franco government in Spain.

According to the reasoning prevailing in the United States, the Nationalist government retains its legal status despite the Communists' *de facto* control of the mainland —as did, for example, the legal governments of countries overrun by Nazi Germany. This is so because, in American opinion, the Chinese Communist government has not met Jefferson's second criterion and has repeatedly violated the third one. In particular, the aggression in Korea charged to China by the United Nations has not been purged by Peking's subsequent actions. Hence the formal grounds for America's continued recognition of the Kuomintang government remain valid. They apply equally to America's stand on the seating of the Chinese Communist regime in the United Nations. This line of argument makes little impression in India. Indians say that these principles were not applied by the United States in comparable cases, including the states of Eastern Europe and Israel. Few, if any, Americans would agree that the recognition of Israel or even of the East European states in the immediate postwar period was comparable to the China recognition question. Secondly, Indians say that in officially negotiating with the representatives of Communist China, as it has done in several situations, the United States government has in effect recognized the Peking government.

So much for the legal question. In political terms, basically the more important, the question is: which Chinese regime should profit from whatever advantages result from the admission of a government to the United Nations and from the carrying on of normal diplomatic intercourse? If diplomatic recognition implied no more than taking note of a *de facto* situation, the extension of such recognition to Communist China would pose a lesser dilemma to many Americans. Actually some Americans argue that under existing circumstances—in which American and Communist Chinese diplomats have negotiated on various issues both indirectly and face to face—the United States gains little from withholding recognition. The opposing group, emphasizing China's part in the Communist bloc, is appalled at the measures being taken within China to fasten totalitarian controls over the whole society and is persuaded that China's remorseless drive to increase its national power, as well as Chinese action in Korea, indicate expansionist ambitions. This view has received widespread governmental and public support in the United States and was endorsed by both major political parties in their 1956 national platforms. Recognition, after all, does have strong political overtones. America's pledged word is seen by many Americans as bound up with continued support of Chiang Kai-shek. This view is reinforced when the recognition question is considered as part of the global struggle to build up the strength of other nations to resist the further expansion of the Communist bloc.

It is sometimes argued that recognition by the United States and the admission of Communist China to the United Nations would enhance the prospects of peace by giving China wider opportunities for international contacts and so weaning it away from Russia. Most Americans, though only a few Indians, doubt that relations between the two strongest Communist states would be much affected by the diplomatic actions of other states. Mostly, American opinion holds that recognition would have the opposite effect, that of encouraging the Communist powers to pursue an even more intransigent course. Far from accepting an American offer of recognition in the spirit of moderation and adjustment, the present leaders in Peking would, they believe on the basis of past experiences, exploit this step toward conciliation as a great political victory over the free world and as a stepping-stone to fresh expansion of their power.

Thus the prevailing American line of reasoning runs counter to the Indian approach. To Indian government leaders the international acceptance of Communist China would have symbolic importance as a recognition of the new status of Asian peoples in world affairs. More urgently, they hold that peace in Asia depends partly on the recognition of the government of Communist China, which rules over nearly 600,000,000 people and controls a vast land mass. Since almost all issues relating to peace and war in East Asia must affect and be affected by Communist China, they argue, drawing China into normal diplomatic relations with the world's capitals is essential if these issues are to be settled by negotiation and compromise.

It is clear that on the issues of recognition and of seating of Communist China in the United Nations India and the United States have not seen eye to eye. From time to time various suggestions have been made for breaking the deadlock but none of them has had much reality. Thus on occasion it has been suggested that Security Council membership be revised so that the permanent seat now held by Nationalist China would be given to India. This is not acceptable to India nor is it in accord with its friendly relations with Communist China. Another proposal has been that both the Communist and the Nationalist governments be recognized and both be accepted as members of the United Nations. In this manner international representation of the Communist regime would be secured without forcing the withdrawal of the recognition that the United States and a large number of other countries continue to give to the Nationalist government. At present there is however little support for such a proposal from any side.

Recently both the Indian and American governments have been acting as if it would be better to let the issue lie dormant for the time being since there seems to be no acceptable way out of the present impasse. This course of "agreeing to disagree" also serves the desire of both India and the United States to preserve peace in East Asia. Furthermore, the issues of recognition and United Nations membership are part of a larger context which must itself change before any real new developments can be expected on these two issues.

Formosa

There is for example little expectation that the questions of recognition and United Nations membership can be resolved so long as the status of Formosa remains in contest. The history of the island makes possible differing claims. After centuries of independent existence Formosa was seized in the seventeenth century by Chinese imperial forces and was a part of China until the Japanese annexed it at the close of the Sino-Japanese war of 1894–1895. In

1943, at Cairo, Roosevelt, Churchill and Chiang Kai-shek agreed to restore to the Republic of China the territories that, as the communiqué put it, Japan had "stolen" from China and to expel Japan from all other territories "taken by violence." Manchuria, Formosa and the Pescadores were expressly mentioned as areas to be returned to China. This decision was reaffirmed at the Potsdam Conference in 1945. By 1951 however, when the peace treaty with Japan was signed, Chiang Kai-shek had been driven from the mainland and had established the Nationalist government on Formosa. The peace treaty stripped Japan of its title to that island but did not provide specifically for its disposition. On the basis of these facts and on the premise that defeat on the mainland did not extinguish its jurisdiction, the Nationalist government has disputed all challenges to its sovereignty over Formosa.

The Chinese Communists have argued their case from the position that the People's government, by its mainland victory, became the successor government of China and inherited sovereignty over all of China's territory including Formosa, thus placing the Kuomintang regime in the status merely of a rebellious opposition. According to this line of reasoning, Communist action against Formosa would be of the nature of a domestic police action, much as the mainland regime regards the establishment of its control over Tibet.

Being the sole remaining base of the Chinese Nationalists, the only center with which non-Communist or anti-Communist Chinese—whether on the mainland or in Southeast Asia or in other parts of the world—can now identify themselves, strategically located in the Western Pacific, and favored with one of the highest standards of living in Asia, Formosa is obviously the core of the Nationalist government. It is also important symbolically and practically to the Communists, and herein lies the threat to peace which has caused continuing anxiety in India and in the United States. The Communists have repeatedly declared their intention of "liberating" Formosa, peacefully if possible but by force if necessary. In 1955 they emphasized the point by building up airfields, supply dumps and other military facilities along the Fukien coast opposite Formosa. More recently they have tried to sway individual Nationalist leaders by holding forth the prospect of negotiation and by promising honorific posts under Communist rule to any Chinese on Formosa who would contribute to the "liberation" of the island. Meanwhile, the Nationalist government has made every preparation to prevent the Communists from seizing Formosa and the off-shore islands. Occasionally the Nationalist leaders also talk of the reconquest of the mainland.

The Indian government does not recognize the Kuomintang regime on Formosa and would, indeed, not be averse to seeing the end of a regime which depends so heavily on American support. In part, this attitude is based on the danger of war inherent in the present situation; in part, it is a result of the Indian feeling that the open and substantial American support to Chiang's regime represents a new kind of imperialism in Asia—much as does, in Indian eyes, American aid to Syngman Rhee and to the Diem government in South Viet Nam. It is assumed in India however that American opinion would not willingly accept a Communist seizure of Formosa and this for a number of reasons: the consequent strengthening of the Communist bloc, the effect on non-Communist Chinese everywhere of such a resounding Communist victory, the increased strategic threat to the Philippine Islands, and the extensive "liquidations" that would be likely to take place. It should however be pointed out that after much-publicized talk in the United States of "unleashing" Chiang's forces against the mainland, the obligations of the United States under the Mutual Defense Pact of 1954 were limited to cooperation for the defense against aggression of Formosa, the Pescadores, the island territories in the West Pacific under United States jurisdiction, and "such other territories as may be determined by mutual agreement." Although in supplementary notes it was agreed that Nationalist China controls not only Formosa and the Pescadores but also "other territory" (i.e., the offshore islands), with respect to which it also possesses "the inherent right of self-defense," the notes continued,[1]

In view of the obligations of the two Parties under the said Treaty, and of the fact that the use of force from either of these areas by either of the Parties affects the other, it is agreed that such use of force will be a matter of joint agreement, subject to action of an emergency character which is clearly an exercise of the inherent right of self-defense.

In the present state of world tension, control of Formosa by a friendly government is seen by many Americans as important for the security of the Philippines, of Japan, and finally of the United States itself. It is also seen in the United States as important in the longer run to the security of Southeast and South Asia.

Both India and the United States have advised the two Chinese regimes not to break the peace over or from Formosa. It has so far not been possible however to work out any acceptable "solution" of the Formosa question. For this a *sine qua non* would be to provide assurances against any use of force on either side. The idea of an independent Formosa is from time to time explored. The first problem that would arise would be the identity of the rulers. Should they be the native Formosans or the Chinese now resident there? The claims of both could be pressed. The second consideration would be that an independent Formosa could probably be established only if it were neutralized, a possibility that would require the renunciation both of Nationalist ambitions to return to the mainland and of Communist determination to "liberate" the island. It would also probably be necessary to provide outside help to ensure further development of the Formosan economy. Overlaid with difficulties as it is, this solution may have some positive features, if pursued gradually, peaceably and without undue pressure. It may be, of course,

[1] *Documents on American Foreign Relations, 1954* (New York: Harper, for the Council on Foreign Relations, 1955), pp. 363-364.

that with the passage of time, the two Chinese governments will reach some sort of settlement on their own. For
the present however there seems to be no alternative to
the continuation of the existing and uneasy situation. It
is to be expected that in line with their general concept
of international conflict, of the nature of the two Chinese
regimes, and of India's proper role, Indian policy-makers
will continue to try to bring the Chinese Communists and
the United States closer together.

Tibet and India's Northeast Frontier Area

Let us turn now from the comparison of Indian and
American policies toward the two Chinese governments to
those areas—Tibet, Korea and Southeast Asia—in which
the expansion of Communist Chinese influence, or the
threat of its expansion, have caused serious concern to
either India or the United States. The interaction of Indian and American policies in this sphere has hit close to
concepts of security as well as to a number of other basic
concerns.

The sharpest differences that India has so far had with
Communist China arose over the manner in which the
Communist regime in 1950 extinguished the ancient
though partial autonomy of Tibet and brought that country within its military and political control. That the
Chinese government exercised suzerainty over Tibet had
long been internationally accepted. On the other hand,
India had inherited the special privileges obtained by the
Younghusband expedition which the British had sent into
the area early in this century in an effort to make Tibet
into a buffer state between Russia, China and India. Under
this previous arrangement, India had from 1947 maintained a Political Agent in Lhasa, specified trade agencies,
and certain postal and telegraph facilities within the borders of Tibet, as well as a small military contingent in the
town of Gyantse.

When in August 1950 the Communist regime announced

its intention of sending troops into Tibet, the Indian government strongly urged it to settle the question of its relations with Tibet peacefully. Nevertheless Chinese troops marched to the border of Tibet and later into all the main centers of the country. The Indian protest was prompt and emphatic; in an exchange of notes India described the Chinese action as deplorable. The Chinese reply was a complete rebuff to the Indian position. Stating that Sino-Tibetan relations were a domestic matter in which "no foreign interference would be tolerated," the Communist government went on to point out that the Chinese troops had been sent "to liberate the Tibetan people and defend the frontier of China" and that Indian reaction must have been "affected by foreign influences hostile to China." The Indian government categorically denied the last of these allegations and was not pleased by the insulting implication that Chinese troops had entered Tibet in order to "defend" its borders. Nor were the implications for long-term Indian security particularly consoling, as large Chinese forces displaced the unarmed Tibetan levies.

After China had intervened in the Korean war India, feeling that the greater world danger lay there, did not press the Tibetan matter. Indeed it was not clear that there was anything further that India could have done about the Chinese presence in Tibet, except to protest through diplomatic channels. However, in spite of later Indian efforts to minimize the importance of Tibetan developments, it is clear that the implications to Indian security have not escaped careful notice in New Delhi. By their penetration into Tibet the Chinese have moved much closer to India, and through their road and airfield construction they are drastically changing what was long considered an impregnable fastness. And, in part because it is now installed in Tibet, China is in a position to put heavier pressure on the Nepali government through economic and political means. In so doing it has increased its capacity to penetrate into a zone which India has considered particularly important to its own security. As Prime Minister Nehru put it in Parliament in December 1950: [2]

Our interest in the internal conditions of Nepal has become still more acute and personal, because of the developments across our borders, to be frank, especially those in China and Tibet. Besides our sympathetic interest in Nepal, we were also interested in the security of our own country. From time immemorial the Himalayas have provided us with a magnificent frontier. Of course, they are no longer as impassable as they used to be but are still fairly effective. The Himalayas lie mostly on the northern border of Nepal. We cannot allow that barrier to be penetrated because it is also the principal barrier to India. Therefore, much as we appreciate the independence of Nepal, we cannot allow anything to go wrong in Nepal or permit that barrier to be crossed or weakened, because that would be a risk to our own security.

Much the same type of concern applies to the security of other sections of the northeast frontier as well. In its use of security measures along its borders India has applied every means that it had at hand from purely domestic measures and the strengthening of its protectorates over Sikkim and Bhutan to agreements with and advice to the buffer state of Nepal. Because this frontier area is little known to most American readers it may be helpful to indicate the action of the Indian government along this frontier, even though the information may be quite familiar to Indian readers.

There are first of all the measures taken within the jurisdiction of the Indian government. Thus in the northeast frontier area within India the government has been building roads and airstrips. Indian army detachments are on the alert at various points. In 1953 a special section was established in the Ministry of External Affairs to extend political control over the wild border areas, often with the help of Indian army units. There has been vigorous action taken against rebellious tribesmen. In addition the Indian

[2] *Jawaharlal Nehru's Speeches, 1949–1953* (Delhi: Ministry of Information and Broadcasting, 1954), p. 176.

government has taken action to guard the border between Ladakh (Kashmir) and western Tibet while the government of Uttar Pradesh has, with the help of the federal government at New Delhi, established special constabulary forces to patrol and control the frontier in the Kumaon area. Outside influence, as represented by foreign missionaries, is under constant scrutiny.

In the case of Sikkim, which, like Bhutan, is regarded by the Indian government as within the country's international frontier, India, by a treaty concluded on December 5, 1950, shortly after the invasion of Tibet by Chinese forces, acquired "the right to take such measures as it considers necessary for the defence of Sikkim or the security of India. . . ." (Article 3) including the right to station troops within Sikkim. India also received full control of Sikkim's external relations "and the Government of Sikkim shall have no dealing with any foreign power" (Article 4). India's control over defense and external relations was further buttressed by an exclusive right to construct, maintain and regulate the transportation and communication facilities of the princely state. In return, the Maharaja of Sikkim was to receive an annual subsidy of 300,000 rupees ($63,000). By an earlier treaty signed on August 8, 1949, Bhutan too had ceded control of its external relations to India in return for an annual subsidy of 500,000 rupees ($105,000).[3] Thus in India's relations with both Sikkim and Bhutan the status of protected and protector inherited from the British was continued, but more clearly and sharply defined.

With Nepal, India's relations are more complicated and delicate. A treaty which, like the Indo-Sikkim treaty, was signed in 1950 provides for consultations between India and Nepal in the event of an external threat to the independence or security of either of them. India's keen interest in the development of democratic institutions in Nepal was shown clearly in 1950 by its policy toward the incidents

[3] *Indian Yearbook of International Affairs* (University of Madras: 1953), v. 2, pp. 295-296 and 319-322.

that led to the overthrow of the feudal government controlled by the Rana family. Since then India's interest has been evidenced by continuing advice as well as by the economic and military help India has given to the Nepali government. In political affairs Nepali politicians have frequently turned to the Indian representative for advice, but they have as frequently fulminated against him when the King of Nepal has sought his advice. In spite of pressing needs at home Indian experts have been dispatched to Nepal to train an army and a civil service, to build schools where almost none existed before, and to build roads with the help of the Indian army. The financial efforts India is making in Nepal are shown by the fact that in 1954, India spent close to eighteen million dollars in that country for development purposes and that these expenditures have continued. India also plays an important role in the foreign trade policy of Nepal.

These facts will suffice to indicate the nature of the Indian goal in Nepal: to protect Indian security through the development of a government capable of performing needed services and of carrying out needed reforms, as well as one that will look to India for the protection it may need. Although India sponsored Nepal's application for membership in the United Nations and encourages Nepali participation in international conferences, it is interesting to note that India has consistently favored the accreditation of "concurrent" representatives to Nepal who serve simultaneously in India and Nepal and make their homes in India.

Many Americans consider Indian thinking on security matters to be sharply divided in several compartments. Where it is a matter of the security of India's borders, the Indian government has used all the means available, including military means, to ensure so far as its resources allowed that Indian peace and integrity should not be endangered by direct attack. These Indian efforts to keep out hostile influence from its border areas recall to American eyes a familiar and logical pattern.

A critic of Indian policy might say that the pattern of Indian policy toward its protectorates and Nepal differs little from policies toward buffer states that India has severely criticized when other nations have been involved. He might add, however, that Indian effort in this area is designed to enhance the stability and security of India, to promote the maintenance of present balance in Asia and to prevent the growth of foreign influence in the areas along its borders. There would seem to be little doubt that in the interests of self-defense India is obligated to resist as strongly as possible any attempts by these states to move away from its influence. Within this context Chinese Communist efforts in 1956 to develop closer influence in Nepal through economic and *Pancha Shil* agreements as well as through other means can only be disturbing to policymakers in New Delhi.

To return briefly to Tibetan developments, they have had a certain significance in Indian-American relations. In Indian eyes the response of the Indian government demonstrated a readiness to move decisively when basic security interests were involved and to move by a combination of economic, political and military measures not unlike those adopted by the United States against somewhat similar threats to its security. To this extent Americans could see certain parallels in Indian and American policies. Americans have at times been puzzled by the Indian reluctance to admit these parallels. Furthermore, Americans tend to wonder that this approach is not extended by India to a broader appreciation of the function of international positions of strength as counters to evident Chinese Communist expansionist tendencies. Indians on the other hand take pride in the fact that the Indian government has developed its diplomatic ties with China, and presumably, its diplomatic influence in Peking, in a way that has not been possible for the United States in its relations with those countries from which it sees a threat to its security. In the American view, however, the effective value of that influence has not yet been put to a severe test.

Korea

Developments in Tibet posed a threat of considerable magnitude to Indian security to which India responded with the countermeasures noted above. On the other hand the events of 1950 and after in Korea—which in American eyes in varying measure involved the security of Japan, of the Philippines and of the United States—were significant to Indians almost exclusively because they raised the specter of a world war. Thus the American view that the North Korean aggression, *if not repelled,* posed an ultimate threat to all of Asia, and that it represented a chapter of a world-wide Communist plan of expansion, was not widely accepted in India. Yet because of its concern with preventing the Korean conflict from spreading into world war India was far from being a mere spectator in the conflict. Indeed some of the key principles of Indian policy involving the nature of the United Nations and of great power relations were put to the test as the war progressed.

Before the North Korean attack in June 1950 the Indian government and Indian opinion had hardly been interested in Korean matters except that the government had protested, as a member of the United Nations Commission in Korea, against the "power politics" of both the Soviet Union and the United States, policies which in the Indian view kept the country from being unified. The United States had on the other hand found itself unexpectedly but closely involved in Korean affairs. Thus before the war's end the United States had advocated the formation of a united Korea under the temporary guidance of a four power trusteeship. At the end of the war it accepted—supposedly only for the purposes of receiving the Japanese surrender—what it thought was to be the temporary division of Korea at the 38th parallel. American expectations in 1945 and 1946 that the formation of a unified provisional government for all of Korea would proceed rapidly were frustrated by the Soviet determination to entrench a Communist regime north of the dividing line. After failing in its repeated efforts to negotiate a settlement bilaterally with the Russians, the United States in 1947 placed the Korean matter before the United Nations, which recognized President Syngman Rhee's government. North Korea ignored all United Nations attempts at settling the country's future on the basis of free elections and national unity.

In spite of some fears in the United States and some United Nations warnings that attack from the north was in preparation, American assistance to South Korea was limited to some economic help and to the training of lightly armed local security units. By June 1949 the United States had withdrawn all military forces except for a training mission. It refused President Rhee's repeated requests for heavy weapons for fear that they might be used offensively. In January 1950, when Secretary of State Acheson defined the American "defense perimeter" in the Western Pacific, he did not include Korea in his listing of countries that the United States was committed to defend against Communist attack.

When the North Korean forces launched their well prepared attack against South Korea on June 25, 1950, both India and the United States were greatly perturbed. Was Moscow behind the move? Would Korea become another Greece? Was the attack aimed at the elimination of American influence from the Asian mainland or was it the first step in World War III? On American initiative the Security Council was immediately called into session. Both India and the United States supported the Council resolutions of June 25 and 27, 1950, passed in the absence of the Soviet delegate. Since January the U.S.S.R. had boycotted the Council because of its failure to act favorably on the Soviet proposal to transfer China's permanent seat to the Communist government.

The resolution of June 25 declared the North Korean attack to be a breach of the peace and asked North Korea to cease hostilities immediately and withdraw its forces north of the 38th parallel. The resolution also directed the United Nations Commission in Korea to report on the implementation of the resolution and called on all United Nations members "to render every assistance to the United Nations in the execution of this resolution and to refrain from giving assistance to the North Korean forces." On the same evening, in response to President Rhee's urgent appeals and consonant with the Council resolution, President Truman arranged to give military supplies and help to South Korea under the Mutual Defense Assistance program. On the next day the United Nations Commission reported to the Secretary-General that the advance of the North Koreans was so rapid that the operation might end in a few days, rendering the question of a cease-fire and the withdrawal of North Korean troops "academic." By noon of June 27 the American government ordered American air and sea units to "give the Korean Government troops cover and support" while the Seventh Fleet was instructed to proceed to the Formosa Strait in order to prevent the conflict from spreading to that area and to keep the rival Chinese forces from attacking each other.

Later on that same day the Security Council passed a resolution sponsored by the United States requesting that "the members of the United Nations furnish such assistance to the Republic of Korea as may be necessary to repel the armed attack and to restore international peace and security in the area." In a precedent-making decision the United States committed forces to fight under United Nations command in order to prevent the aggression from succeeding by default. It was a difficult time for American policy-makers. They knew that the North Korean attack could be stopped only if the United States chose to use those of its own forces present in or near Japan and chose to do so quickly. They knew from bitter experience that United Nations directives would by themselves mean nothing to the North Koreans who had disregarded them repeatedly and deliberately and that therefore these directives would have to be backed by the United States with American lives until other members of the United Nations could bring up elements of their armed forces from far-off places. It was therefore up to the United States to take or not take the quick action that alone could prevent the North Korean attack from becoming a complete triumph for aggression.

Although the Indian representative on the Security Council voted for the two basic resolutions, India distrusted the implications of the use of armed forces by the United Nations, as these resolutions had of course not had the support of the Soviet Union or Communist China. India also feared that the mounting of a campaign against the North Korean aggression might touch off a major war. The Indian government believed that the proper function of the United Nations was to offer conciliation and mediation rather than to organize the enforcement of its directives, unless the enforcement measures had the support of all the major powers. For this same reason the Indian government did not support American-sponsored efforts to give the General Assembly a degree of jurisdiction over matters of peace and security such as the Korean conflict, so that it could act in the event of the Security Council being paralyzed through conflict among its permanent members.

To the United States organized international armed resistance seemed the only way left to stop the aggressor and demonstrate that aggression does not pay. The Indians feared the implications of this approach. They emphasized instead an appeal for the restoration of peace through negotiation and mediation for which purpose, by implication, Prime Minister Nehru had offered India's good offices early in July. India again urged the seating of Communist China in the United Nations on the ground that no stable solution of the Korean question by the United Nations was possible unless the United Nations secured the support of the Chinese Communist government. India did not join the United Nations armed action partly because of domestic security and economic considerations and partly because of its desire to keep itself free to act as a mediator between the two sides. As a token of sympathy for the South Korean people, it sent an ambulance unit.

This Indian approach created a good deal of irritation in the United States, where it was regarded as unrealistic and ineffectual and criticized as undermining effective United Nations action. As a result, India came to be widely regarded in the United States as "neutral on the Communist side." To Americans it seemed inconsistent for India to oppose aggression, to advocate compromise with the aggressor and to criticize those countries that were making great sacrifices to prove that aggression should not be rewarded at the expense of those attacked.

As the United Nations forces threw back the North Koreans and approached the 38th parallel, the question arose as to whether the fighting should stop at this line or whether the counteroffensive should be carried into North Korea in order to force the aggressor to cease fighting and come to an agreement. Most South Koreans and many Americans believed that the war begun by the North should end in uniting the two halves of Korea, in accordance with the United Nations resolutions of 1947, 1948 and 1949. India opposed this action, pointing out that the original resolution of June 1950 had called only for repelling the aggressor from South Korea. It also warned the United Nations and the United States that the Indian ambassador in Peking had been informed by the Chinese Communist government that the approach of the United Nations forces, composed largely of American troops, toward the Yalu river was considered by the Chinese as a threat to their security and would be opposed.

The American view was that if the North Korean army could enjoy an unmolested sanctuary north of the 38th parallel, it could rebuild its forces at leisure, refuse to accept any political settlement and at a time of its own choosing renew its attack on South Korea. The United States delegation pointed out that the final goal of the United Nations was to establish a "unified, independent and democratic government in the sovereign state of

Korea," and that the barrier to the accomplishment of this goal was the action of the Communist-backed North Korean regime which had for five years rejected all United Nations proposals for unifying the country and had recently committed a deliberate aggression. Most Americans did not believe that an attempt to secure a unified Korea by the action of the United Nations constituted a threat to any country, including Communist China.

Nevertheless, Chinese "volunteers" entered Korea on November 5 and the danger of the war spreading became suddenly very acute. As the United Nations troops reeled back toward the southern tip of Korea under the massive attack of fresh and well-equipped Chinese Communist forces, it appeared for the second time as if the Communist powers were on the verge of conquering all of South Korea in defiance of the United Nations. As the dimensions of the Chinese Communist drive became clear, the increasing demand in the American press and Congress for the use of atomic weapons to stop them and to rescue the United Nations forces greatly alarmed India as well as Great Britain and France, and Prime Minister Attlee flew to Washington on December 3 to confer with President Truman. Their joint statement, which invited China to negotiate for a Korean settlement, was interpreted as a decision to seek a settlement through negotiation and to refrain from using atomic weapons for fear of bringing Russia into the war. On December 5, the Asian-Arab "neutral" group in the United Nations, including India, issued an appeal of its own to China to halt its advance at the 38th parallel and to begin peace negotiations. Nine days later the General Assembly accepted a resolution initiated by the same Asian-Arab group urging the opening of negotiations for a cease-fire in Korea. This proposal as well as a second cease-fire appeal, adopted on January 13, 1951, were rejected by the Communist Chinese government, whose forces were still advancing. The American delegation now insisted that the United Nations condemn the Chinese aggression. India opposed this resolution. It argued that the Chinese Communist government had warned the United Nations forces not to advance toward its Korean frontier, a warning which the United Nations command had not heeded. Therefore the Chinese action should not be described as an act of aggression. However, the United Nations General Assembly by a vote of 44 to 7 with 9 abstentions adopted the American-sponsored resolution censuring Chinese aggression. India voted with the Soviet bloc against this resolution.

Throughout 1951, in spite of rebuffs from China and the Soviet Union, the Indian government—together with other Asian nations and on occasion with representatives of the Western nations—continued to work for a negotiated settlement between the United Nations and the Chinese Communists. Continuing to insist on the necessity for admitting Communist China to the United Nations, the Indian government welcomed the truce talks that began in July 1951, and in late 1952 made a major effort at mediation by seeking to break the deadlock which had arisen over the post-armistice exchange of prisoners of war. Meanwhile, as the conflict dragged on during 1951, a "Great Debate" took place in the United States. On one side were those who felt that the fighting should be carried into China in order to cut off the channels by which massive supplies and fresh divisions were moved into North Korea and to interdict the use of Manchurian airfields by the Chinese as a privileged sanctuary. On the other side were those who felt that such action would contain the gravest danger of touching off a world war, that at the least it would commit the United States to a struggle of unknown duration to overthrow the Chinese Communist government, and that by committing available American forces in Asia it would give the Soviet Union an unparalleled opportunity to expand. In addition it was clear that the military effort in Korea, if expanded to Chinese territory, would no longer receive the wide moral support of the United Nations or the manpower support of the United Nations members which had provided contingents for backing

United Nations actions against the aggressors. While the controversy was going on in the United States every American reaction to United Nations peace proposals was conditioned by these wide-ranging arguments and by strong resentment over the role of Communist China in prolonging the fighting in defiance of the United Nations.

The basic purpose of the United States continued however to be the achievement of an acceptable peace, one that by not rewarding the aggressor would help to deter later aggressions elsewhere. When the Soviet government indicated in June 1951 that the Chinese Communists were at last willing to accept some sort of compromise, instead of seeking to drive the United Nations forces into the sea, the United States was glad to take advantage of this shift and entered into negotiations. As far as Indian-American relations were concerned, the long drawn-out armistice negotiations revealed two issues on which India and the United States took opposing stands: the scope and make-up of the proposed political conference and the conditions of the repatriation of prisoners of war. While the United States held out for a conference on the Korean settlement to be attended by the nations that had borne the fighting, India argued that Korea was only one among many issues in the Far East and that chances of a settlement in that area would be enhanced if other interested but nonbelligerent Asian countries also took part. Since, as it turned out, the political conference was never held, irritation over this difference was short-lived. On the question of repatriation, Indian government and public opinion was at first inclined to give credence to the Chinese assertion that many tens of thousands of Chinese and North Korean prisoners were refusing to be repatriated because they had been subjected to "intimidation and pressure." India regarded American and South Korean estimates of the prisoners' temper as less than disinterested. When the deadlock over repatriation delayed the cease-fire, India offered a plan which the United Nations adopted in December 1952 and the Chinese accepted four months later by which the issue was to be resolved after the cease-fire. However, the later experience of an Indian representative as the Chairman of the five-power Neutral Nations Repatriation Commission which had custody of the prisoners and supervised their interrogation, brought home to some Indian leaders and to a section of public opinion the persistently dilatory and obstructive tactics of the Communists at Panmunjom and led to an acceptance of the fact that tens of thousands of Chinese and North Koreans were actually unwilling to return to their Communist-ruled homelands.

Taken as a whole, the Korean war experience without question somewhat estranged India and the United States. Indian opposition to the American course in Korea reached its peak at the northward crossing of the 38th parallel, but was a continuing feature of Indian policy from 1950 to 1953, just as American criticism of India continued strong through that period.

Both Americans and Indians wanted peace but they differed over the best way to secure it. Their short-term goals were far apart. India pressed steadily for an immediate, compromise peace to reduce the threat of a bigger war spreading across East Asia, whereas the United States, desiring to avert a new world war, strove for a settlement that would discourage Communist aggression anywhere. Indian and American estimates of Communist China's role clashed. To the United States it was an aggressive and obdurate regime persistently acting against the United Nations. Most Indians believed that the Chinese Communists were basically committed to peaceful domestic development and had been drawn against their will into the Korean war to protect vital interests.

The means which each nation had available also differed. India had important influence and contacts for negotiation between the belligerents in Korea as the only major Asian non-Communist and nonbelligerent country which maintained active diplomatic relations with Peking. India had no military capacities that could affect the actual fighting significantly, whereas American forces supplied the major and essential factor of power in the effort to resist aggression. It is not surprising that their perspectives on Korea differed radically and that relations between India and Communist China tended to improve when American opposition to Communist China hardened. As the war came to an end, however, India and America drew a little closer again. India's firmly fair conduct of the interrogation of war prisoners gained American respect while the experience gave Indian leaders a more intimate view of Chinese Communist actions.

Southeast Asia

In Southeast Asia, as in so many areas of interest to both nations, India and the United States have pursued the same basic goals: genuine independence and genuine peace, together with a healthy economic and social development. But in matters of concrete action the two governments have as often as not failed to see eye to eye and have in fact often pursued contrary and even contradictory policies. For India the future of Southeast Asia is of vital importance. It is also an area susceptible to the application of major Indian tenets of peace and war. In Indian eyes the theme of Asian resurgence—including Chinese Communist resurgence—continues to dominate India's attitude toward Southeast Asia. On the other hand the United States emphasis has since 1950 been placed on the danger inherent in the growth of Communist pressure on Southeast Asian nations. American policy has sought to deal with this pressure through a combination of political, economic and military measures. This difference in focus has created much tension in Indian-American relations, a tension that has sometimes been unduly compounded by lack of information and by misunderstanding. A prime example has been policy differences over Indochina.

From 1945 on, Indian opinion was at all times highly critical of French government attempts to reinstate authority over Indochina and to split the ranks of the nationalists. But the Indian government refused to recognize either Bao Dai or Ho Chi Minh, although most Indians regarded the Communist leader as a more sincere spokesman for nationalist aspirations. The French attempts also failed to win much American support, although the American attitude was tempered by a reluctance to interfere in the conflict to a point that might undermine the vulnerable and crucial position of France in Europe. Even though many Americans were skeptical of the ability or willingness of the French to establish effective cooperation with the nationalist forces in Indochina, Washington channeled its military and economic aid through the French government until mid-1954, when France itself recognized the independence of Viet Nam, Laos and Cambodia. From 1950 on, the United States provided much of the supplies and other aid to Indochina. When, with the end of the fighting in Korea, Chinese Communist military supplies and support began to flow in increased amounts to Indochina, the United States also stepped up its aid to the French, although at the same time it continued to urge them to take a number of steps to strengthen the position of the nationalists. This American policy lent itself to criticism by both sides. In particular, many newspapers and groups in France attacked the United States loudly for allegedly "conspiring" to destroy the French position in Indochina.

Meanwhile, the situation in Indochina deteriorated. By 1954 it was clear that the Bao Dai regime had proved ineffective. A new regime under Premier Ngo Dinh Diem was just beginning to take its first steps in the southern half of Viet Nam. Fighting had broken out in hitherto peaceful Cambodia. In Laos the Communist-dominated Pathet Lao forces were challenging the established government. And the Communist forces in the north, strengthened by the considerable training and equipment received from Communist Chinese sources, had captured the French forces at Dien Bien Phu, where, the French had announced, they would make their last military effort to defend Indo-china.

As the military situation of the French went from bad to worse, Indian diplomats sought to convince all concerned of the wisdom of settling the crisis by conference and with the participation of Communist China. Such a conference was finally fixed for April 25, 1954, at Geneva. On the eve of the conference the French in a desperate bid asked Britain and the United States for air cover over Dien Bien Phu, or—in other words—to enter the war. The request was rejected. The British government preferred to see whether the Geneva conference might provide a solution; the American government felt that a last minute and limited intervention would not save the desperate French position, in view of their failure since 1945 to work out a basis of genuine cooperation with the nationalists.

By the agreements at Geneva, in which Indian diplomats played an important though unofficial role, France undertook to withdraw its troops from Indochina and recognized the independent status of Cambodia, Laos and Viet Nam; Viet Nam was however left divided at the 17th parallel. American opinion was not sanguine that the agreements had laid the basis for a lasting peace and neither South Viet Nam nor the United States government signed them. India welcomed the agreements because they achieved the withdrawal of imperial forces from a section of Asia, achieved international recognition of the independence of several Asian states, and could bring peace to an area that had been torn by fighting for nine years.

Thereafter, with the French no longer dominant in Indochina, two main questions concerning Indochina have continued to affect the development of Indian-American relations: future relations between the two rival governments of North and South Viet Nam, and reactions to the increased Communist influence. Although India refused to recognize either Ho Chi Minh or Diem, its sympathies as evidenced through diplomatic and newspaper comment for long seemed to lie with Ho, whom it has regarded as representing indigenous nationalism rather than fulfilling the ambitions of international communism. The United States on the other hand has at Diem's request given his government considerable military and economic help in order to strengthen the government of South Viet Nam against the possibility of attack from the north and to build up its administration and economy. The United States has also supported Diem in his refusal to join with North Viet Nam in holding elections in both halves of the country for the purpose of creating a single unified government. South Viet Nam maintains that there can be no genuinely free election in Communist-ruled North Viet Nam. The Indian government on the other hand has repeatedly stated its conviction that the election should be held in both halves of the country.

India and the United States also seem to disagree over the dangers of a further extension of Communist rule to South Viet Nam, Laos and Cambodia. As early as March 29, 1954, Secretary of State Dulles [4] warned that

The propagandists of Red China and Russia make it apparent that the purpose is to dominate all of Southeast Asia. Southeast Asia is the so-called "rice bowl" which helps to feed the densely populated region that extends from India to Japan. . . . The area has great strategic value. . . . Communist control of Southeast Asia would carry a grave threat to the Philippines, Australia, and New Zealand. . . . The entire Western Pacific area . . . would be strategically endangered. . . . The United States feels that that possibility should not be passively accepted but should be met with united action.

India on the other hand has based its policy on the agreements reached at Geneva and has devoted its efforts to keeping them in effect on the assumption that this approach offers the best possibility of preserving peace or at least preventing the outbreak of open military conflict.

Although India has declined to commit its forces to the

[4] *Department of State Bulletin*, v. 30 (April 12, 1954), pp. 539-540.

defense of Southeast Asia in the military sphere, it has been willing to help in the onerous tasks of settling various issues once the fighting has stopped. As in Korea, this was true in Indochina where India has borne the heavy responsibility of chairing the International Commissions for Supervision and Control for Viet Nam, Laos and Cambodia. Faced with extremely difficult tasks involving refugees, military matériel, preparations for general elections in Viet Nam, as well as other tangled issues in Laos and Cambodia, the Commissions were limited by the Geneva agreements to functions of supervision, investigation and recommendation. They were dependent on local authorities—including Communist authorities—for the preservation of order and the opportunity to execute their duties. In addition, the membership of the Commissions was bound to increase the difficulties they would have in trying to act effectively. The Canadian and Polish members held irreconcilable views on many issues and it fell to the Indian chairmen to attempt to strike a balance between them. This they did fairly successfully, always with the basic goal in mind of preventing any breakdown of the Commissions. Inevitably there was much that the Commissions could not see or could not deal with, and their reports evoked severe criticism in some quarters. Both Ho and Diem refused to cooperate in carrying out those decisions that ran counter to their views. Given its support for the government of South Viet Nam and its own refusal to sign the Geneva agreements, the United States has viewed Diem's protests with more sympathy than the Indians could. With the passage of time, however, at least some segments of Indian opinion appear to hold a more favorable impression of Diem and he is no longer so consistently regarded as nothing but an "American tool."

Within the wider context of Southeast Asia similar differences in emphasis have gradually brought India and the United States to adopt contrasting positions on how best to protect the independence and peace of the peoples of the area. Both recognize the deep roots of instability in

Southeast Asia: the variety of separate cultures, the under-developed economies, the lingering aftereffects of colonial domination, and the presence of some twelve million Overseas Chinese whose allegiance is the object of a three-cornered rivalry between the countries where they reside and the Nationalist and Communist Chinese regimes, both of which claim them as Chinese citizens on the basis of *jus sanguinis*.

Indians and Americans have also been aware that externally inspired pressures have complicated the domestic difficulties of Southeast Asian countries. Guerrilla movements led by Communists have at various times sought to overthrow the governments of Burma, Indonesia and the Philippines. In 1956 Communists also showed their capacity, in Burma and Indonesia, to increase their strength through the use of parliamentary institutions. In Burma there has been much alarm over the incursion of Chinese Communist troops across ill-defined frontiers, and the Thai government too has been exercised over Chinese Communist ambitions, expressed in the formation of a "Free Thai" government on the territory of Communist China. The long continuing guerrilla warfare in Malaya cannot be entirely dissociated from its Chinese Communist backing. Indonesia has tried but unsuccessfully to reach agreement with Peking over the ambiguous status of Overseas Chinese in Indonesia. Naturally, the newly-independent governments of Southeast Asia are fearful of the growing strength of Communist China and of some of its policies. At the Bandung Conference of 1955 and since, the Chinese Communist leaders have sought to weaken these fears through reiterating their peaceful purposes and offering support against "Western imperialism." However, the fears are far from having been put at rest. India and the United States have had to consider how they could be most helpful to the Southeast Asian peoples in this situation as well as how they could best protect their own national interests in maintaining peace within this larger area.

Indian and American capacities to assist the independent national regimes of Southeast Asia differ markedly. Both recognize that Southeast Asian countries need substantial economic assistance. India, though itself hardpressed, has made certain contributions in aid. Thus it has coupled its aid program to Nepal with a loan to Burma and has canceled the debt arising out of Burma's separation from India in 1937. American economic and technical assistance programs of a major character are functioning in the area, through the Colombo Plan and through direct agreement with the governments of the Philippines, Indonesia, Thailand, Laos, Cambodia, South Viet Nam and, recently again, in Burma. Some informed Indian opinion is aware of these American efforts and their constructive goals, though misinformation and prejudice on this subject are still widespread.

In major policy terms, India has two instruments in Southeast Asia. It regularly seeks to concert its policies with those of other nations, both through bilateral diplomacy and through the workings of the Colombo and Asian-African groups. In spite of the many differences that divide, say, Pakistan and Ceylon from India, these efforts have great value, particularly in United Nations bodies. But India's main instrument is the concept of *Pancha Shil,* considered the best assurance against aggression, infiltration or subversion. India has signed a network of *Pancha Shil* agreements—with China, Indonesia, Ceylon and Cambodia as well as Egypt, Saudi Arabia, the Soviet Union and others. In the prevailing Indian view, the *Pancha Shil* approach is both morally and practically the best path to peace. It is felt to combine the most idealistic ingredients of Western thinking on the conduct of civilized nations with the highest principles of Indian thought. The moral opprobrium that would attach to any nation violating the *Pancha Shil* pledges is regarded as strong enough to save smaller nations from the constant threat of conquest or war and therefore to relax tensions that would otherwise feed on themselves. Also, because only the great powers have the military capacity required to oppose major aggression, the *Pancha Shil* are seen as the only assurance on which weaker nations can rely without becoming "entangled" with a great power or being involved in the "cold war." Under Gandhi's leadership India experienced the power of moral force in its struggle for independence. Transferring this experience to a wider scene, many Indians agree with Prime Minister Nehru that "it is a choice between the *Pancha Shil* and the H-Bomb." Furthermore, by the *Pancha Shil* and by its friendly policy toward China at the Bandung Conference and elsewhere, the Indian government has hoped not only to bring about a wholesome relaxation of tensions in general but also to erect policy barriers that would guard against possible Chinese "nibbling excursions" along its ill-defined borders as well as against political adventures outside of China. In other words, through the *Pancha Shil* the Indian government has hoped to help preserve the independence and peace of areas around China by creating an aroused public opinion whose alienation the Chinese Communist regime would not care to risk. This policy fits well with general Indian concepts of the manner in which international affairs should be conducted and it also does not call for the expenditure of men, money and materials that India does not wish to spare from its internal development plans.

Most Americans are skeptical of the effectiveness of declarations such as the *Pancha Shil* in deterring aggression, infiltration or subversion. They cite the Burmese border difficulties with Communist China, the sad fate of the Kellogg-Briand Pact of 1929, and the failure of the Yalta and Potsdam agreements to assure the independence of East European countries and of Korea. Some Americans assert that the Indian government is able to make the *Pancha Shil* a "pillar of policy" because other countries are simultaneously providing a military deterrent against Communist expansion. In Southeast Asia as elsewhere postwar experiences have impressed on Americans the conviction that an essential deterrent to aggression, infiltration and subversion is the advance demonstration that they will not pay because they will not be allowed to succeed. The debacle in Indochina in 1954 convinced the American government of the seriousness of the Communist threat in Southeast Asia, and led it to found the Southeast Asia Treaty Organization in September of 1954, together with the Philippines, Thailand, Australia and New Zealand, Pakistan, Britain and France. Together with the Australian-New Zealand-United States pact and the American bilateral mutual defense agreements with the Philippines, Formosa, South Korea and Japan, SEATO was intended to serve notice on Communist China that aggression in Southeast Asia would be strongly and collectively opposed. Concurrently the SEATO signatories also adopted a Pacific Charter proclaiming anew their devotion to equal rights and self-determination; to the orderly development of self-government; to cooperation in economic, social and cultural fields; and to the prevention of any attempt to subvert the freedom, sovereignty or territorial integrity of the countries in the treaty area.

If there are reasons to be skeptical of the *Pancha Shil* approach, many feel that SEATO is also inadequate. Some would call it harmful. The Indian government and much of Indian private opinion have in very strong terms decried SEATO as a dangerous development, one which brings Western powers back into a region that has only recently thrown off Western domination, increases tensions in the area by stimulating China to take countermeasures, drains into military channels the resources that are badly needed for economic and social development, and encourages regional rivalries and animosities. Some also doubt that SEATO is an effective deterrent to aggression because it calls for consultation rather than for automatic retaliation in the event of trouble. Others are bothered by the fact that the membership of the organization does not include several of the most important countries of Southeast Asia.

So long as India continues to criticize the American policy in Southeast Asia as increasing the danger of war, and Americans continue to dismiss the *Pancha Shil* as at best impractical, a common approach to the region can hardly be expected. The existence of two somewhat competitive linkages, SEATO and the *Pancha Shil* group, is not very satisfactory. And yet, emotions apart, the two approaches do not necessarily work at cross purposes. Many nations in both groups have the same purpose: the freedom and security of Southeast Asia. The division between the two does not extend to all their activities; members of both groupings work together in such cooperative undertakings as the Colombo Plan and the Economic Commission for Asia and the Far East, as well as on many issues that come before the United Nations. With this common goal and with growing conviction in one another's good faith, India and the United States may be able in the future to consult more fully and fruitfully on Southeast Asian problems, even if their differences over the role of China and the aims of communism continue.

A Look Ahead

The widely separated perspectives from which India and the United States approach the "China Question" have led them to adopt conflicting positions on two major issues: the status to be accorded Communist China and the international security measures to be promoted in the vicinity of China. India actively seeks China's friendship for several cogent reasons. China is a large neighbor whose current development is a symbol of renascent Asia. It is also a major military power pursuing economic, social and political goals that are fundamentally competitive with those of India. If India did not pursue a policy of friendship with China, many Indians feel, it would find it harder to retain its posture of nonalignment with any grouping of major powers. More important, the country would then be saddled with defense commitments far more extensive than the present security arrangements along its northern frontier and in Nepal. Any such commitments could seriously impede India's economic development plans on which depends its own ultimate stability. Thus it appears likely that India will continue to emphasize friendly diplomacy in the face of indirect or veiled Chinese expansion. It appears unlikely that India will materially change its posture toward Communist China except in the face of direct provocation.

Very different considerations—attachment to the Chinese Nationalist government, the Korean war experience, suspicion of a Sino-Soviet axis with aggressive ambitions—determine American policy in Southeast Asia and toward China. It would seem that only a change in the Far Eastern situation, in Soviet-American relations or in United States relations with its allies could lead to any fundamental shift in United States policy toward China and Southeast Asia. But while India and the United States apparently must agree to differ at least for a time, it is significant that some of their specific actions have not been alien to the other in some important respects. Thus for example when India regarded its security challenged by China's strengthened grip over Tibet, it pursued in Nepal a combination of economic, political and military measures paralleling measures adopted by the United States in some areas where it has perceived security threats to itself. If, as this suggests, one difference between India and the United States lies in divergent judgments of what threatens both them and international peace, further experience of Chinese policies may bring their assessments into fuller concordance and thus draw them closer to each other.

Chapter 6

ECONOMIC PROBLEMS IN INDIAN-AMERICAN RELATIONS

THE ECONOMIC problems that figure most prominently in
Indian-American relations are those connected with the
opportunities and limitations of foreign aid programs in
general, and with Indian efforts and development in particular. They are basically concerned with the extent to
which and the manner in which American capital—whether
private or governmental—is to participate in this development.

There are also, of course, trade problems, always complicated and difficult enough. Both India and the United
States trade more with third countries than with each
other. The trade between them has grown since Indian
independence, but its expansion is handicapped by many
factors. Although it has been able to draw on the pooled
dollar earnings of the sterling area, India has suffered from
a dollar shortage that inhibits imports from the United
States. Increasing domestic demand coupled with problems of production and transportation limit the volume
of goods India can export. Additional handicaps, such as
limited commercial contacts, restrict the amount of Indian
exports that can be placed on the American market. The
long-standing commercial and financial ties of Indians
with the sterling area play a considerable role in India's
foreign trade. Thus, even under the best of circumstances
Indian-American trade is likely to increase slowly. The

increase may bring with it new problems as well as new benefits. But at present trade problems are not sufficient to explain the urgency and political fervor with which economic relations between the two countries are discussed in popular forums and government circles. Perhaps in part this urgency and fervor are due to the fact that the general and often vaguely felt differences on political and other matters find a concrete focus in the discussion of economic matters and the implementation of economic policy.

The stake that India has in the success of its development plans is obvious. It does not need to be elaborated here except to point out that in the pursuit of their goals Indian leaders have reluctantly come to the conclusion that because development requires more imports than they can currently pay for, large-scale foreign help—though marginal to the total effort—is nevertheless of crucial importance and should be encouraged. It should be encouraged whether it comes in the form of government aid or of private investment, provided it is willing to stay within the framework of Indian planning. It should also be encouraged—and this ties in with the Indian world outlook—from whatever nation may offer it; in this respect as in so many others, no official distinction is made between Communist and other states.

The reluctance with which Indian leaders and opinion alike have reached these conclusions has been concentrated largely on a lingering suspicion of Western "economic domination," of political "strings" attached to such participation, a fear that acceptance of large-scale help may curtail Indian independence, a fear lest such help become a "crutch" on which the Indian people will come to rely as a substitute for their own effort, as well as a fear that acceptance of such help from the West will lessen the force of India's voice in international affairs. Nevertheless, Indian experience with Western participation in its development plans has on the whole been good and these fears and suspicions may be considered background factors rather than matters for present consideration.

The American interest in the success of Indian development plans is difficult to express in any single formula. It will help to set the matter in perspective to remember that many of the problems and much of the reasoning concerning India are part of the broader issues facing the United States as it attempts to deal with the need for help to less developed areas all over the world. Just how much aid should be given, and for what reasons, are matters which have been under active study by the government and which have drawn heated debate in the Congress and by the public. Obviously, no nation will continue indefinitely to offer help unless it feels that its national interests will be served thereby; this is as true of India in its help to Nepal and to Burma as it is of the United States in its help to India.

There is thus a definite correlation between the attitude of Americans toward help to India and their estimates of the effect on American national interests of India's national and international policies. Those who feel that the Indian policy of nonalignment is in practice an aid to the Communist nations are likely to oppose any increase in help to India or indeed any help to India at all. There are a number of variations on this theme but this is what it comes to basically. There is on the other hand much opinion in favor of help to India which emphasizes the American national interest in the existence of an independent and democratic India and which holds India to be the strongest supporter of democracy among Asian nations. In this view a specific political or diplomatic stance taken by India's leaders is of comparatively little importance so long as the domestic development of India proceeds along democratic lines while in foreign affairs the nation remains genuinely independent.

Two basic aims seem to guide those Americans who favor continued or increased American help to India. There is first of all the desire—extending back to the early war years and antedating the emergence of the Communist threat—to see the healthy development of the so-called underdeveloped areas in the hope that this will add to the economic and political health and stability of the world and thus also to the health and stability of the United States. This desire is reinforced by the conviction that the frustration of the "revolution of rising expectations" can lead only to upheaval, instability and other undesirable results. Those who hold this view feel therefore that the need to aid economic development exists apart from the Communist threat and would have under any circumstances demanded the attention of the United States in its own self-interest.

Adding an urgency and acuteness to this understanding has been the emergence of the Communist threat. That a large number of Americans have come to feel the need for foreign aid, particularly to Asia, as a result of this multi-pronged danger cannot be denied. Furthermore, this danger has in large part determined the form and amounts of aid and has in most instances led to the weighing of aid to a specific country both against the Communist pressures bearing upon it and against its anti-Communist record. It is those countries that have been fighting acute military threats that have called forth the largest and most dramatic American aid efforts. Thus, South Korea, Formosa and South Viet Nam are the Asian countries that have received the most concentrated aid for the simple reason that they have been and are in mortal danger. Furthermore, since much so-called military aid is in reality also economic aid, American thinking has not made as much of a distinction between the two as have Indian critics.

To many Indians this approach to distribution of aid has seemed distasteful and short-sighted, mainly on the ground that aid given in advance of crisis to areas with potentially critical problems could achieve so much more and at less cost to the people involved. Although many Americans would agree in principle with this position, they would also feel that—given the course of events in Asia

since 1950—critical situations have again and again confronted American policy with critical decisions. At least in
both South Korea and South Viet Nam this responsibility
of decision was accepted, even though perhaps it could
have been accepted at an earlier and less dangerous stage.
In spite of Indian criticism it is of course clear that much
American aid, including aid to India, has been based on
the principle advocated by most Indians: that of giving
aid to help healthy development and to avoid critical and
acute situations.

Although by far the most attention in the United States
Congress has been concentrated on help to those Asian
countries willing or forced to fight Communist expansion
through military means, and although there has been a corresponding reluctance in some quarters to grant a non-
aligned India much assistance, the emergence of the Communist threat has also had what might be called a favorable impact on American opinion concerning aid to India.
Because of this threat, more people in the United States
assign a higher priority than before to American participation in Indian development and are willing to contem-
plate a considerable expansion in aid. Specifically, it is
clear that the outcome of the "demonstration race" into
which India has been forced by Chinese Communist actions and plans will have wide repercussions in Asia and
Africa. These reactions will affect the security of the
United States. In this view the American stake in the success of Indian development plans is very high.

Concrete issues of economic policy arise against a background of general understanding—or misunderstanding—
between India and the United States about some of the
major features of the character of each country's economic
system and economic activity. There is in India considerable suspicion of American capitalism, as of private capitalism in general. Although the high standard of living of
the mass of the United States population is comparatively
well known in India, at the same time the picture of capitalism in operation held in even generally well-informed

circles is colored by experience during the colonial period and replete with clichés taken from Karl Marx and the Fabian Socialists. Many Indians know little if anything of the social responsibility of private enterprise in America, of the numerous governmental controls on all levels, and of the ramifications of the social security system, among other relevant points. A better acquaintance with the American economic system resulting from serious on-the-spot study could do much to dissipate some of the misinformed assumptions that exacerbate relations—and not only economic relations—between the two countries.

On the other hand, American experience has led most Americans to favor private enterprise wherever it is possible. This method of operation has worked well in the United States, it has proved amenable to social goals and to the establishment of a high standard of living and of human dignity, and it was born of and fosters a valuable spirit of initiative. Furthermore, it seems to many Americans that the diffusion of economic and of other important decision-making power which, to a significant degree, has accompanied the American private enterprise system, is in itself a valuable asset to the vitality of a political democracy. In such a setting it is perhaps not surprising that there is frequently a hostile reaction to economic programs, such as the Indian, which claim to be "socialistic" or to governments that avow their intention of moving toward a "socialistic pattern of society." To Americans it also seems that there is a certain amount of confusion in India itself concerning the socialistic goals that were adopted by Parliament in 1954 and that have been elaborated in a number of subsequent pronouncements. Various Indian spokesmen seem to speak with different voices when it comes to explaining the character of this future order. While Americans may take comfort from some of these statements, they are disturbed by others.

In the Indian point of view, these American criticisms and suggestions all too frequently seem to have little relevance to the Indian scene. Indian leaders are under pressure, both domestic and external, to build up the base of a healthy economy with the greatest speed possible. In their effort they are attracted toward Socialist measures. They feel that their experience with the private entrepreneur has also not been especially sanguine. And they would be the first to acknowledge that they are still feeling their way toward the Socialist goals that were adopted by Parliament in 1954 and at other times.

In fact, the general goals of Indian policy have been set by the constitution. It says, for example, that the state is to strive to promote the welfare of the people by securing a just social order. In order to accomplish this, the constitution continues, the state is to see to it that all citizens have an adequate means of livelihood, which is their right; that the ownership and control of the material resources of the community are so distributed as best to subserve the common good; and that the operation of the economic system does not result in the concentration of wealth and means of production to the common detriment. By themselves, these statements would not be a cause for misunderstanding. Welfare and justice for the individual are goals which are close to American thinking. The differences come—as they so often do—in execution.

Given the intellectual background of most Indian leaders, the magnitude of Indian tasks and the impatience of the Indian people for visible results, it is not surprising that the largest role in economic affairs has been given to the state, and this without much protest from private enterprise. Indeed, the constitution speaks of the "state" as accomplishing the objectives which it outlines. Nevertheless—although much American opinion can understand the Indian point of view—the extremely large role given to the state is alien to Americans in times of peace and creates a number of misgivings. These are, generally speaking, only in part assuaged by various statements of Prime Minister Nehru pointing out that the Indian government is interested not in the wholesale nationalization or confiscation or destruction of private enterprise but in the creation of new enterprise and production by both government and by private business. The Indian government has for example cooperated in the establishment of certain organizations designed to help Indian private business. The National Industrial Development Corporation (1954), a registered private company with a paid-up capital provided entirely by the government, is among other things to start basic new industries, help the growth of ancillary industries in the private sector and ensure maximum use of its existing equipment and skills. The National Small Industries Corporation (1955) is another private registered company with capital entirely supplied by the government whose purpose is to help certain small industries employing not more than one hundred persons in securing orders and in improving methods of production. The Industrial Finance Corporation of India was established in 1948 to provide medium and long-term loans to industrial concerns, and in 1955 the Industrial Credit and Investment Corporation of India was initiated as a private registered company for the purpose of helping in the development of private industrial enterprise. The total resources of the latter amount to about $36,000,000, made up by an issue of ordinary shares to investors in India, the United Kingdom and the United States; a deferred and interest-free loan by the government of India; and a loan from the International Bank for Reconstruction and Development.

These measures have not however overcome the sense of uncertainty in much American opinion as to the direction in which the Indian economy is traveling and particularly as to the results that can be expected from the definite Indian prejudice in favor of government action in most economic spheres of direct national importance. In turn, much Indian opinion feels that American criticisms of Indian economic planning and the role of the state in economic life represent nothing so much as an "insular fondness" for the system which has worked well in the United States but which, it is often felt, has little relevance to the Indian scene. It is true that on occasion some

Americans have criticized India in terms that might give the impression that they would wish India to become a carbon copy of the United States in economic matters. But such critics are in a minority.

It is particularly important that Indians and Americans understand each other's economic positions and viewpoints because with its second Five Year Plan (1956–1961) India entered upon a critical period in which the barriers to success are many and in which unobstructed Indian-American understanding on economic matters is of considerable importance. This is so because the second Five Year Plan which is, with its heavy emphasis on industry, considerably more ambitious than the first, is being carried out under very difficult conditions, prominent among which are a continuing inflation, a drastic lack of foreign exchange, and a critical undersupply of jobs for a labor force that is expected to increase by some ten million *new* job-seekers within the next ten years. The understanding help of the United States can be particularly telling in the matter of foreign exchange, which would in turn have wide repercussions in all other aspects of India's plans for economic development.

Given the magnitude of the tasks the Indian government has set and its increasing need for help in certain aspects of these tasks, as well as the American interest in Indian success, the importance of the two major economic issues that often divide the two countries can hardly be exaggerated. These issues are: conditions of private investment and matters of government aid. While it is convenient to consider private investment and government aid together, it is also important to keep in mind the significant distinctions between them. Government aid is provided in response to the judgment of national interest described above. Private investment, though it may be encouraged by governmental action, depends on the attitudes and judgments of advantage made by businessmen in numerous separate enterprises. While both United States government aid and private investment supplement India's foreign exchange supplies and usually provide a transfer of real resources, there are apt to be important differences in the relations they set up and the role they play in the mobilization and use of resources inside India. (The contribution of private organizations should not be overlooked of course but in terms of size and the magnitude of projects that may be undertaken, their role, though possibly seminal, cannot be considered on the same plane.)

Taking private investment first, most Indian opinion seems agreed on the desirability of increased private investment from abroad, provided that that investment takes place in "capital overhead" or in manufacturing industries within India and within the allocations of the Five Year Plans. In the Indian view excellent conditions have been provided for foreign investment. Foreign businesses that have been able recently to conclude agreements with the Indian government seem to find their position satisfactory.

Yet, little American private capital has come to India. The bulk of new private American investment in India since 1947 has been contributed by the petroleum industry and only a small fraction has come in other fields that India also needs to develop. Indian opinion explains this situation as a result of American "fussiness" and a desire for privileges that the Indian government is not prepared to grant because they would result in too great a disparity between the Indian and foreign investor. Some Indian opinion also holds that American private capital has such good investment opportunities at home or in Canada and Latin America that it would at least for the present not come to India in substantial amounts no matter what inducements the Indian government might wish to offer within the limits of the Five Year Plans. Some Indians and many Americans feel however that this point has not been proven and that it would be worthwhile to explore further the reasons for which American private capital has been relatively reluctant to enter into economic activities in India.

Apart from the uncertainties that have been mentioned

earlier about the direction in which political control of
the Indian economy is moving, the American business-
man's reluctance to invest in India has arisen also from unfamiliarity with Indian working conditions and the Indian
market, the apparent scarcity of trained labor, uncertain
and involved labor regulations, and the restrictions on
private business promulgated in 1956. One example of
these restrictions is the provision of the Second Statement
of Governmental Industrial Policy that several industries—
such as aluminum, machine tools, drugs, fertilizers—which
have elsewhere been susceptible to development by foreign
investment will in India be "progressively state-owned."
Another which it is feared could have adverse future implications is the provision of the Companies Act of 1956 en-
titling the Indian government to place governmental
nominees on the boards of directors of managing agencies
and to determine the permissible levels of compensation
for executives. These actions are explained in India by
the unhappy experience during the colonial period, but
many Americans believe that such policies may in the long
run stifle the growth of a risk-taking, active group of Indian
private business leaders who could be of crucial importance to Indian economic development. They also believe
that the regulative measures taken by the Indian government in relation to all private investment may prove to
be so severe as to discourage private investments still more.

Perhaps the question should be raised as to whether for
the time being the Indian government can afford to be as
critical of private investment as it has been in view of
the goals of its Plan. Perhaps Indian long-term aims might
be better served by the creation of a more welcoming atmosphere which would encourage the entry of foreign private investment into those fields where foreign capital
and "know-how" are, in the opinion of the Indian government, urgently needed. Perhaps also such changes would
make it possible to explore in concrete terms and through
concrete discussions just what possibilities might exist and

under what conditions more foreign private capital—particularly American capital—would come into India.

In any case however the magnitude of the Indian need for foreign exchange during the second Plan—the figures that are bruited about are over a billion dollars—makes the need for foreign government aid inescapable no matter how much private investment might increase. As in the matter of private investment, voices are from time to time raised in India against accepting foreign aid, but by and large the need for aid, and in increased amounts, has been accepted by government leaders. Similarly, despite voices that have been raised in the United States against foreign aid in general and against aid to India in particular, the American government and people have accepted aid to India as in the American national interest. In ten years nearly a billion dollars of American government money have been spent or obligated to assist the development of the Indian economy. Each appropriation has been the result of careful negotiation between the Indian and American governments to assure both the donors and the recipients that the money would contribute effectively to their common ends. In spite of some theoretical differences that have emerged in the process and some differences over day-to-day operations, the record shows clearly that Indian-American experience in bilateral aid programs has been uniformly good.

It is within the context of that basically successful record that the different approaches to governmental aid in India and in the United States can be examined. For one thing, Indian leaders would prefer as a matter of principle to receive aid from international organizations or via international arrangements such as the Colombo Plan on the expressed assumption that such aid is more likely to be free of "political strings." It is also felt that the participation of both donor and recipient on an equal basis in a grouping in which there is more than one recipient (and more than one donor) is both less demanding and more likely to lead to the success of the viewpoint of the recipients. Channeling a large part of foreign aid through the United Nations commends itself to much Indian opinion as the soundest course.

As is well known, the United States has taken a somewhat different point of view. It participates in a number of international technical and other aid programs, notably those of the United Nations and its specialized agencies. In recent years about half of the contributions to the United Nations Expanded Technical Assistance Program have come from the United States. Some American funds are channeled to underdeveloped countries through the International Bank for Reconstruction and Development, and the International Finance Corporation. The United States also participates in the Colombo Plan. There is however relatively little support in the United States for the suggestion that the bulk of American aid should be distributed through an international agency, such as the proposed SUNFED. There is doubt whether such an agency would actually be free of political influence and stratagem. As a matter of fact, it seems clear to many Americans that an international program in which the Soviet Union was an active participant would be very likely to become a political football in a short time. This was America's unhappy experience with the fundamentally humanitarian UNRRA program. Furthermore, there is a fear that a large-scale international program might lack strict standards concerning the most productive use of aid, while the participation of a large number of recipient countries within the decision-making process might—though not necessarily— serve to initiate an undesirable "pork barrel" approach. And finally, there are domestic American considerations as well. Congress is traditionally jealous of its control over the "purse strings" and the foreign aid programs have been no exception. Without a doubt Congress views with disfavor proposals for new and large international funds to which the United States would be expected to contribute heavily but in which it would probably not have much say as to how the money was to be spent. Nevertheless—although present government policy does not reflect this—the idea of an international aid fund is not without appeal to some sections of American opinion.

Realistically speaking, the bulk of American aid can be expected to be given in the future as it has been in the past, on a bilateral, government-to-government basis. The realization is spreading in India that expansion or continuation of American aid will build on the bilateral patterns that have already been established in Indian-American relations.

The specific form of aid has on occasion also caused some irritation between India and the United States. Putting aside the statement sometimes made in India that the United States has an obligation to aid the underdeveloped countries—which is not accepted in the United States—there has been some feeling and even resentment in India at the great contrast in size between the Marshall Plan for Europe and aid given to Asia. Although American aid has recently swung increasingly toward Asia this feeling still exists as a background factor. It is particularly important in feeding the accusation that a Europe-oriented United States was willing to give much larger sums to Europe than it is to Asia.

In the United States the history of aid programs is interpreted differently. After World War II primary attention was for good reason centered on the acute problems of European reconstruction, while concrete help toward Asian development, which was for a time thought to be less urgent, was given in smaller sums. In recent years however aid to Asia has increased and the United States is restudying its aid programs. But it cannot be denied that the problems and financing of development in Asia are far different from those of reconstruction in Europe. Some of the factors of production, such as for example a pool of highly trained labor and management, have not yet even come into existence in underdeveloped Asian countries. Thus the capacity to absorb aid rapidly and use it efficiently and without undesirable side effects has differed materially between Europe and Asia. India—with its considerable industrial base already in being—is more fortunate than most of its neighbors in this respect but even so American aid to India has been of a different order of magnitude from that to Europe.

These economic factors, the total aid commitments accepted by the American government in a given year, the particulars of each recipient country's stated needs, and the direction of bilateral negotiations, all come into the determination of the amount of American aid to be offered to each assisted country each year. The situation is thus more complex than an assertion of "favoritism to Europe" would indicate. It is of course not surprising that the underdeveloped countries are impatient and want to move ahead as fast as possible while the donor nation is more conservative and cautious in its reasoning.

There is the further criticism that American aid—in addition to not being large enough—is subject to Executive and legislative processes that reduce its potential effectiveness. Funds for aid have been provided on a year-to-year basis. The direction and amounts of aid have thus been dependent on an annual interplay of differing interests. This has left the recipient nation—it is held—in a position in which it cannot count on aid for projects over a period of years and leads to uneasiness as well as resentment. President Eisenhower has sought Congressional commitments of funds for a longer period with only partial success. Long-term loans can, however, be made under existing arrangements.

Criticism of aid policies reflects also the political differences of the two countries as to the nature and strategy of the cold war. On the one hand, one need only mention the matter of American aid to Pakistan. On the other hand, there is some American concern over Indian acceptance of Soviet aid.

Not all Americans believe that United States aid policies should be strongly influenced by whether or not a particular country also accepts Soviet aid; some regard the "competition" as likely to reveal to the recipient the inherent contrasts between Soviet and American aid policies. As for the considerable number of Americans who are troubled by the fact that India accepts Communist aid, it is not so much a question of the mere fact, though at times this can play a part in irritating relations, or of the present amount, which is relatively modest. On the ground that the Soviet Union is a totalitarian country which uses all its resources in a total effort to bring about its goal of world revolution, some Americans are concerned about the opportunities for subversion which such aid might provide, in the future, if not now. There is also concern over the future effect on Indian thought and policy that may result from the training in the Soviet Union or by Soviet experts of young Indians who may later rise to positions of importance. While the American concern lies mainly with the future, the Indian reply is couched in terms of the present. In the predominant Indian view the American fears are unjustified as the Indian government has been careful as far as possible to keep such contacts in balance with contacts with other sources. Here is still another chapter in the differences between India and the United States on the meaning, methods and nature of communism.

What can be said in summary of the problems that are involved in Indian-United States economic relations? It is clear that in terms of their national interests both nations have something to gain from good economic relations. The United States has a stake in the success of India's economic development. India in turn needs American support. In general, relations in this field have been good even though a certain amount of irritation on both sides does exist; this rises to a high point usually during the very frank debates in the United States Congress over the granting of further aid. Perhaps as the characteristics of the American system of government become more familiar to more Indians, much of the present dismay and offense will disappear.

With continued Indian economic development and barring any drastic political changes, Indian-United States trade may over the years be expected to increase—a development that would seem to promise mutual profit and a possible strengthening of bonds in other fields. At present such trade, though increasing, is hampered by the inconvertibility of many currencies into dollars which causes India to conserve scarce dollars for goods urgently needed in development plans and to make other purchases elsewhere.

As far as private investment is concerned, it is worth repeating that a more sympathetic consideration by the Indian government of the doubts and difficulties experienced by American investors may have fruitful results in terms of benefits to Indian economic development. And evidence of such reconsideration might well serve to improve the tone of general Indian-American relations.

In matters of government aid both governments would do well to consider in what ways they might modify their policies—without giving up essential goals—to fit more closely with each other's needs. There is nothing wrong in admitting that both countries are subject to domestic political compulsions as well as to economic realities in their policies on foreign aid and economic development. Nevertheless, as mentioned earlier, the over-all record of Indian-American relations on aid questions has been excellent. It was a harbinger of further future successes that in 1956 the two countries found a way to overcome some of the restraints that had troubled them by concluding the Agricultural Commodities Agreement. Under its terms the United States agreed to sell to India commodities of which that country stands in great need and of which the United States has a surplus. Payment by the Indian government will take place in rupees, most of which the United States will then lend to India for development purposes. The sums loaned will be repaid over a period of years. Some of the rest of the money will be given to India in development grants and the remainder will be spent in India by the United States government. Although this pattern will not suit all the problems that have and will continue to come up, nevertheless it shows that the two governments are capable of negotiating carefully, hard-headedly and with confidence and that they are able to overcome many of the deficiencies that each feels in the other.

Chapter 7

COLONIALISM

THE ISSUE of colonialism has been a pervasive and at times an intensely emotional factor in Indian-American relations. Whether it will continue to be so is open to question. For one thing, the successes of the movements for national freedom have substantially outmoded the issue in Asia and considerably reduced its dimensions in Africa. For another, the gap between the approaches of the two countries has narrowed, for reasons which we shall examine. Yet a gap remains. It is in part a matter of policy, often expressed in differences over timing or over whether a country's readiness for independence should be determined exclusively by the metropolitan power or through United Nations machinery. In perhaps larger part it is a matter of emotions, important because emotion-laden reactions to remaining colonial issues have a tendency to outrun policy differences and so to augment the strains between India and the United States that have been discussed in earlier chapters.

Both the United States and India agree that colonialism is a moral problem and both are traditionally and fundamentally anti-imperialist. However, they inevitably approach current colonial problems from different perspectives. The Indian anticolonial struggle is still so recent as to need no extended discussion: it is part of the personal experience of millions of Indians including the national leaders. Given this background, there is in India intense impatience because some non-European peoples remain

155

under the rule of European governments. In Indian eyes the fight against this evil overshadows almost all other world issues.

As a matter of principle the Indian government expects all nations that it considers "right-minded" to take a firm and clear stand against such colonialism. As a matter of policy it expects them to back this stand with decisions of the highest priority. India has made a cardinal policy of developing close relations with other recently independent countries and championing actively the causes of peoples now agitating for political freedom from West European metropolitan powers. The bond of a recently shared experience of dependency embraces most of India's closest present international associations. India's active policy on colonial issues has also given it a leading role in a world issue that affects a vast number of people. It accounts for much of India's international status.

The United States too has a strong tradition of anti-colonialism in which its people take pride: Americans think of their own revolution, of the Monroe Doctrine and its reformulation into an international instrument, of Woodrow Wilson's stress on self-determination, of their encouragement of self-rule in Puerto Rico, and of support to nationalist movements in other dependent areas. At the same time Americans have generally come to the opinion that colonial problems cannot be dealt with effectively without due attention to the serious threat posed by the "new colonialism" of international communism. In policy terms the United States holds that the major responsibility of states not directly involved in the colonial relationship is to help work out decisions which give weight to the interests of both metropolitan powers and dissatisfied dependent peoples—bearing in mind that both have contributions to make to the welfare and security of the world. In trying to achieve this goal, the United States has usually placed more emphasis than has the Indian government on looking into the readiness of a particular area for self-government, keeping in mind the needs and demands of its European allies as they fit into the world security picture, the need to counter the threat of Communist expansion, and the manifold economic, social and political demands made on it throughout the industrially underdeveloped part of the world. Americans feel that other nations that are genuinely concerned with the colonial problem should also recognize and grapple with these complexities.

America's greater caution in supporting colonial causes has created one area of difference with India. A second arises from the opinion generally accepted in the United States, but for years rejected and still viewed with skepticism in India, that the Soviet satellite countries represent a new and undesirable species of colonies. The one view holds that the Soviet Union has consigned its dependent peoples to a new and deadlier form of colonialism which is the more iniquitous because it is expanding today rather than contracting. The other view holds this to be a misreading of the colonial problem and perhaps also of the Soviet system. The full meaning of this difference between India and the United States can be seen in the implications of Prime Minister Nehru's often quoted remark that in "the West the issue of the day is said to be communism; well, to us, it is colonialism."

If the charge is often heard in India that recent American policy on colonialism has been almost entirely determined by the single aim of containing communism, India has been as frequently criticized in the United States for taking an oversimplified view of the colonial problem. In practice, however, India and the United States have come to stand much closer to each other than public discussion would often tend to indicate. In some of the situations which have engaged the attention of both countries, Indian and American policies have been parallel. In others they have been sharply divergent, and on the remainder not in contact. The record indicates how far the United States and India have on the practical level found common approaches to a number of colonial situations.

Past Issues

The extensive liquidation of traditional colonialism is one of the most profound international developments of the present generation. Asian and African countries with a total population of some 645,000,000 have become politically independent since 1939. A number of transitions—in the Philippines in 1946, India and Pakistan in 1947, Burma and Ceylon in 1948—occurred without direct impact on colonial issues between India and America; both Indians and Americans warmly welcomed them. The past instances that most clearly show the interaction of Indian and American policies toward struggling independence movements are to be found in Indonesia, Indochina (discussed in an earlier chapter), and Morocco and Tunisia. Also important is the case of the Italian colonies and of Malaya. Although now of historical concern, these issues invite more detailed examination because of the influence that they exert on the present policies of both India and the United States.

Indonesia. Throughout the Indonesians' bitter struggle against the Netherlands from the defeat of Japan in 1945 to the Hague Round Table Conference of 1948 that resulted in independence for Indonesia, India fully identified itself with the nationalist movement headed by President Sukarno. The Indian government attempted to open trade channels from the earliest moment. In June 1947 it unsuccessfully bade the United States espouse the Indonesian cause and then, with Australia, carried the Indonesian case to the Security Council where it vigorously advocated independence for Indonesia and urged others to do the same or fail to sense "the mood of Asia and Africa." And through the Conference on Indonesia called by Prime Minister Nehru at New Delhi in early 1949 the Indian government underlined the weight of public opinion in Asian and African countries on the matter and stiffened the attitude of the Security Council at a critical point. The Indian government also enforced limited sanctions against the Dutch, among them the denial of flying rights over Indian territory.

United States policy positions were more complex, and in the end perhaps equally influential in assisting the achievement of Indonesian independence. The issue arose just after the war when, for reasons discussed in other chapters, American attention was directed to the revival of Europe and, in Asia, to the problems of Japan and China more than of Southeast Asia. Beginning in June 1947, however, the United States started to play a more active role that frequently reflected compromises between the American interest in reviving the Nazi-ravaged Netherlands and in seeing fair play for the Indonesians. An American *aide mémoire* sent to the Republican government of Indonesia in that month (as an alternative to the action proposed to the United States by India) was, for example, intended to strengthen the nationalists' hand, and did; it was also instrumental in delaying the start of the Dutch offensive. When the "police action" nevertheless occurred and the case came to the Security Council, the United States opposed the Dutch assertion of domestic jurisdiction, offered its good offices to both sides, and worked out compromises which, though weak, enabled the Council to avoid a deadlock and a veto and to establish a three-nation committee to work on the spot in Indonesia. These steps, together with a ban on further sale of arms to the Dutch for use in Indonesia, constituted the first stage of American involvement in the Indonesian case.

In the second stage American public opinion, reflecting popular sympathy for the Indonesian resistance, revulsion against Dutch defiance of Security Council directives, and disgust at the second "police action," stimulated a stronger official position in favor of Indonesia. In February 1949 the so-called Brewster Resolution, presented to the Senate by ten Republican members, called for the stoppage of American aid to the Netherlands until it ceased hostilities in Indonesia, withdrew its troops to the truce lines adopted under the earlier Renville Agreement, and opened "bona fide negotiations with the Indonesian Republic under the terms of the Renville Agreement." The State Department was able to persuade the critical Senators not to cut off aid to the Netherlands only, it is reputed, after Secretary of State Acheson had pressed the Dutch to agree to transfer sovereignty by the end of 1950 to an Indonesian state of which the Republic would be a constituent element. At the Round Table Conference in 1949 the Indonesian negotiators had the support of the United States as well as of India and of various other countries.

The points to be noted are that the policies of India and the United States gradually grew closer as the Indonesian case was exposed in its full complexity, and that both countries contributed effectively to Indonesian independence; true, they proceeded differently because of the different instrumentalities at their command and the relation of the Indonesian dispute to their respective international interests and commitments. In India this parallel has been slow to be observed. Even recently it has been argued there that the United States attitude toward the Indonesian Republic changed only after—and presumably because—the United States government had become convinced that Indonesian leaders were anti-Communist and were receiving international sympathy. This appears to be an oversimplified analysis of a policy-forming process which was certainly influenced by these considerations but which also clearly resulted from humanitarian, moral and emotional factors, as well as from the gradual mobilization of public opinion on this issue.

Morocco and Tunisia. The granting of independence to these two countries in 1956 followed years of violence and of negotiations between the French and the nationalist leaders. The Indians' desire to develop close relations with the Arab world combined in this instance with the longstanding Indian sympathy for anticolonial struggles to produce a very lively feeling for the North African nationalists. This interest and sympathy found particular expression in the United Nations where from 1952 India—

together with the Arab and other Asian nations—made consistent efforts to obtain United Nations intervention on the ground that "the continued denial of human rights and continued disrespect of self-determination cannot but constitute a mounting threat to the peace." The United States on the other hand—voting with the majority of the Assembly—generally took a more hopeful view of negotiations between the French and indigenous groups and favored postponement of any decision on whether the United Nations should take action in this field.

Without going into details of the North African discussions, which ultimately led to results that both India and the United States welcomed, it is clear that once again Indian-American differences were not over principles but over procedures and timing. Caution—or, as Indian opinion often holds, hesitancy—on the American side was generally interpreted in India as favoritism for a European ally over a nationalist movement which had the moral right to self-rule on its side, whereas Indian pressures applied in the United Nations were often interpreted in the United States as exacerbating rather than promoting the delicate process of arranging a transfer of power without undue damage either to France or to the new North African states. Nevertheless, it is important to note that in 1955–1956 the Indian influence on this issue within the Asian-Arab group was one of moderation.

Former Italian Colonies. By contrast, the negotiations within the United Nations through which Libya and Italian Somaliland came under trusteeships for fixed periods were notable because India and the United States made closely parallel approaches to the problem. The two countries agreed that political independence should be the goal of arrangements made for the former Italian colonies, but that these colonies were not yet ready for independence. Both India and America opposed schemes of governance advanced by Britain, France and Russia while they agreed on a settlement providing specifically how the transition to independence should take place in these two territories.

Malaya. There has been no important difference between India and the United States respecting colonial areas that were moving toward self-government by peaceful arrangements with metropolitan governments. Malaya is a case in point. The Indian government, despite its general posture toward colonialism, avoided badgering the British to quit Malaya. The United States took the same line. The Indian position rested on a belief in the sincerity of British promises to work toward independence and perhaps also on the influence of Commonwealth ties. There was also a fear of the explosive potentialities in Malaya of the plural society that exists there. Thus Americans, like Indians, believed that the problem of Malayan independence was one for the British and the peoples of Malaya to work out for themselves.

*   *   *   *

A recapitulation of the colonial issues which have been resolved in the past decade shows little fundamental difference in objectives between India and the United States. It also shows a greater sense of urgency on the part of India than of the United States in pressing for the liquidation of colonial status.

The American record shows a wider concern for the interests of metropolitan powers and more of an attempt to adjust these interests with those of the colonial areas than has been true of India. There is also a greater stress by the United States—if Indochina was a fair example—on the strategic implications of the transfer of power.

In the first postwar decade the United States has also shown greater preference for exerting influence in direct negotiations with the regimes involved in colonial issues, as contrasted to India's preference for widening the authority of the United Nations in this field. Both countries have in the past given effective assistance in the transition of colonies to independent status.

Contemporary Issues

An estimate of the effect of the colonial issue on Indian-American relations must also take into account the colonial matters that still engage the attention of policy-makers in India and the United States. Here a number of categories may be useful.

First, Indian-American relations are not directly affected by those colonial areas where no strong nationalist movement is pressing for independence—such as in the Belgian Congo, Portuguese East and West Africa, French West Africa, and the trust areas in the Pacific. But even here the two countries' approaches differ to some extent. Thus the United States' economic or other interests in these areas are pursued mainly through the metropolitan powers and there is little disposition to influence relations between the home country and the colony. Where a trust territory is involved, the United States proceeds of course through United Nations machinery. India is more likely to draw international attention to abuses and, where possible, to try to expand United Nations supervision over these areas. Whereas Indians look to an Africa that will be wholly free, they tend to believe that the United States has not been very much concerned with the future freedom of Africa, perhaps because of the economic importance of this continent to its Western European allies and the role of Africa's vital reservoir of minerals in United States security. Here as in other instances there is a countervailing strain of American opinion that regards India as overeager to promote change in Africa and as likely to discount the American ability to adjust to new social and political forces as they arise. These differences, however, are more in the realm of attitudes than of specific present policies.

Second, another category includes several colonial areas that do not appear to be moving toward independence but are under pressure or prospective pressure for absorption by neighboring states. Among these, the cases of Cyprus, Goa, Western New Guinea and Southwest Africa have so far entered into Indian-American relations to some degree.

Cyprus. In this case the disposition has been growing in both India and the United States to let the parties involved work out their own solutions. Although American support for the British position was at times somewhat firmer than India's, and although the Indians seemed to subscribe for a time to the idea of a settlement by plebiscite, the 1956–1957 General Assembly saw both countries voting for peaceful negotiation. As a matter of fact it was India that in February 1957 took the lead in working out the United Nations resolution—patterned fairly closely on the earlier Algerian resolution—calling for the resumption of negotiations looking toward a "peaceful, democratic and just solution . . . in accordance with the principles and purposes of the Charter of the United Nations."

Goa. The closest of all present colonial disputes to India's national interests, Goa represents to India a continuing challenge and provocation. The Indian view is that Goa will inevitably detach itself from Portuguese control. To hasten this desired event, India seeks active international support; fear that NATO will support Portuguese sovereignty over Goa has been responsible for much of Indian criticism of that alliance. Secretary of State Dulles' widely quoted statement of December 2, 1955, on the "Portuguese provinces" raised a storm of protest in India. It is often argued there that if the United States were true to its ideals it would intervene with Portugal to yield Goa. It is the American position that this issue can best be worked out between India and Portugal, if possible on the basis of the consent of the Goans. In spite of considerable domestic pressure, the government of India has continued to seek a peaceful way to bring an end to Portuguese control over Goa.

Southwest Africa. Another issue with colonial overtones has been South Africa's policy on Southwest Africa. Both India and the United States, among other countries, objected when the Union of South Africa in 1946 refused to convert its mandate over Southwest Africa into a United Nations trust territory. Both argued, and in this they were later supported by the World Court, that South Africa was under a moral obligation not to change the status of the territory unilaterally. India pressed the United Nations to declare Southwest Africa a trust territory and sought to bring about a censure of South Africa. The United States was among other countries that felt the first action could not be taken legally and that the censure would drive South Africa into a corner without producing the desired effect. Thus the Indian-American difference here rested on the degree of coercion that the United Nations should be asked to apply against a member nation on this issue.

Western New Guinea. The United States government has not declared support for either Dutch or Indonesian claims to this territory. Indeed there is some question among Americans whether the transfer of the area would result in more than the substitution of one alien domination for another. The Indian government on the other hand would probably not accept the inclusion of the area under the rubric of colonial issues, having considered from the start that the area should have passed to the Indonesians at the time of the working out of their independence. Although the Indian delegation has supported Indonesian claims before the United Nations General Assembly, it has not extended that support to the active level of international conferences, appeals to the United Nations, or other actions that have been taken by India on what have in the past appeared to it to be crucial issues.

Third, there are the areas where nationalist movements are pressing for self-rule against the opposition of the metropolitan government, of which Algeria is an example. Here Indians and Americans again differ more in their approaches than in their ultimate policy goals. In the Algerian question the Indian government has moved from great impatience and strongly expressed anticolonialism to a more moderate recognition that "strong" United Nations resolutions would not necessarily contribute to the solution of the complicated problems involved. At the start of the violent Algerian nationalist struggle India urged the inclusion of the Algerian item on the Assembly agenda. When this was done in 1955, the French delegation carried out its threat to walk out of the meeting. Perhaps somewhat shocked by this development, and in spite of its position on the broad competence of the United Nations in matters considered by some to come under the domestic jurisdiction exemption, the Indian government then led in efforts to induce France to return to the Assembly. And in the 1956 Assembly the Indian delegation supported the compromise resolution which confined itself to expressing a hope that "a peaceful, democratic and just solution" might be found. This resolution was welcome also to the United States, which did not take an active part in the discussions. Throughout, the United States has supported the French argument of domestic jurisdiction and has encouraged French efforts to find "liberal solutions" by peaceful means.

Outside the United Nations, the United States has tried to press both France and the Algerians toward what it regards as more reasonable positions and Americans have resented strongly the Egyptian and other sources of continued agitation and of arms that have come into the area. Indian leaders have in general confined themselves to strong statements urging the quick recognition of the right to freedom which they feel belongs to the Algerians.

It would be wrong to ignore the fact that the different Indian and American accents in the Algerian issue have strengthened stereotypes in India of an America that gives comfort to colonial powers and opposes nationalism and stereotypes in the United States of an India that brushes aside the complexities of some issues that it wishes to see solved immediately. But the more important meaning of Algeria in this context is that it offers a good example of how India and the United States sometimes cooperate more closely in practice than in theory. According to its own lights, each country has tried to influence France

without alienating that nation. Both appear to recognize
that nothing could be gained by trying through United
Nations resolutions to force the French government to
take action in Algeria. The relative concordance of approaches that the United States and India had found by
1955 and 1956 would seem to give hope for more cooperation between them on future colonial problems.

The Prospects

It is clear that the colonial issues of 1956 and 1957
roiled Indian-American relations less than those of 1948.
One reason, of course, is that there were fewer of them.
Apart from that, India and the United States had found
more common ground in seeking solutions of the most
difficult conflicts between European powers and their non-
European dependencies. The strong American opposition
to the Israeli-British-French military invasion of Egypt in
1956 made a profound impression in India, and there was
a perceptible decline in Indian suspicions that the United
States would automatically align itself with its Western
allies on colonial questions. Furthermore, in colonial issues
India as well as the United States had come to depend
mainly on the methods of negotiation and accommodation,
rather than on a direct challenge to the metropolitan
power.

It appears less likely now than before that the United
States and India will find themselves in sharp conflict
over specific colonial issues of the traditional type. There
is no reason to believe that India will not continue to
stand for the fastest possible progress toward independence for all peoples, or to suppose that the United States
will not follow more cautious counsels. Yet these are differences of timing rather than of principle. Still important,
however, are the emotional irritants that affect the moods
in which Indian-American relations develop. Indian public opinion seems deeply imbued with the conception of a
vast struggle between the white Western European im-

perial powers and their allies on the one side and the colored Asian and African peoples struggling to obtain and consolidate their independence on the other. In this dichotomy the United States is generally viewed in India as identified with Western Europe. American opinion also continues to be troubled by the contrast between Indian hositility to Western European imperialism, which is everywhere declining or retreating, and the Indian reluctance to recognize the new colonialism of the Soviet Union. While Indian attitudes can be explained on the historical ground of India's direct experience with Western imperialism and its unfamiliarity with the Soviet system, this does not remove American impressions that Indian approaches to colonialism sometimes serve the political ends of the Soviet Union.

At the same time, some persons in both countries already believe that the real "colonial" problem now facing countries which have encouraged the spread of political freedom in Asia and Africa is of a somewhat different cast. They hold that the postcolonial stability of new nations which started with limited human and material resources for self-rule is a matter of international concern. In their view both the United States and India have capacities and experience that could helpfully be applied to the easing of postcolonial crises. It would be worth investigating what cooperation between the two countries might be achieved toward this end.

Chapter 8

HUMAN RIGHTS

CLOSELY ALLIED to problems of colonialism are questions of human rights. These have entered Indian-American relations in two major ways: through the unfavorable stereotypes created in each country by the social inequalities of the other, and through the human rights issues relating to third countries that arise in the United Nations. Like colonialism, the human rights issue is packed with emotions that sometimes obscure and outrun the actual policy issues involved. Its importance in relations between the United States and India must be judged in terms of both.

There is a wide area of fundamental agreement about the inalienable rights of man which most Indians and Americans share with each other. Expressed by the philosophers of the eighteenth-century liberal tradition, given political shape by the American and French revolutions, and adopted subsequently by many other peoples who rank individual rights high among the conditions of a good society, these rights are imbedded in both the American and Indian constitutions. In general these rights limit the powers of government to interfere with individual liberty. They protect the basis of democracy by assuring freedom of speech and religion, of press and assembly and of participation in the political process under the protection of due process of law. In both countries these rights are justiciable. Allegiance to these fundamental rights of man is one of the shared values that create bonds between India

169

and the United States and that distinguish them sharply from nations living under totalitarian regimes.

In addition to these basic political rights there is a second range of values widely accepted and promoted in both societies but often in ways so different that they have on occasion come to be divisive factors in Indian-American relations. Thus there is wide difference on how best to assure to every citizen the opportunity to achieve a good life free from fear and grinding want. In the United States the emphasis has been placed on self-reliance wherever possible, on a diffusion of federal, state and local power among many units, and on the limitation of the government's role where possible. It has further been felt that the basic civil rights are the ones that were emphasized by the eighteenth-century liberals, that these rights are significant under almost any combination of economic and social factors and that—given these rights—the individual can work toward the attainment of economic and social improvements that have not been, and need not be, mentioned in the basic constitutional law. This approach has worked well in the vigorously growing American society.

The prevailing articulate Indian view is considerably different. Influenced by traditions of state paternalism and rigid social framework, much Indian opinion considers the American concept of a few essentially political rights as inadequate. Thus the Bill of Rights has been adjudged as insufficient to meet the requirements of modern Indian society because it does not provide for the right to work, education, food, housing and social security. In Indian eyes it is the state which must offer the best protection for a very wide range of individual rights which, it is felt, should properly be enumerated in the basic law of the land itself.

Given this background, it is natural that in constitutional terms the Indian interpretation of human rights should be very broad. In addition to most of the rights that are to be found in the American Bill of Rights, the Indian constitution seeks also to ensure the equal status of its citizens in such specific matters as access to public places, abolition of untouchability, protection of minorities and freedom from discriminatory restrictions by the state or in choice of vocation or property holding. In the United States such protections—where they are applicable—are provided mainly by local, state or federal legislation or by the forces of social action.

It is in the statement of the Directive Principles of the Indian constitution however that the Indian emphasis on the government's responsibility for achieving social goals becomes clearest. These principles which—though not justiciable—are regarded as fundamental to the governance of the country and which officials have a moral duty to promote, include, as has already been mentioned, the provision of adequate means of livelihood and ownership of the nation's material resources to subserve the common good—a provision usually interpreted in favor of government ownership. They include also the right to work, to education, and to public assistance; the right to just and humane conditions of work; and the elimination of a concentration of wealth.

Differences over the proper role of government in strengthening human rights, while philosophically important, touch only the fringe of the difficulties that exist. It is impossible to discuss Indian-American relations realistically without reference to the strong antipathy in India to the facts and impressions of racial discrimination in America. Similarly, revulsion against the traditional stratifications and divisions of Indian society cannot be ignored as a factor influencing American attitudes toward India. We need, therefore, to consider the effect on Indian-American relations of the Negro problem in the United States and of the caste problem in India.

The disabilities of the Negro in the United States are widely known in India to be one of the acute problems of contemporary American society. The Negroes are, of course, not the only minority group in the United States. But the success of the "melting pot" in transmuting immigrants from all parts of Europe into an egalitarian American society has focused attention in America and abroad on whether the American belief in equality transcends the limits of the white race and is applied fully to the Negroes. The problem is seen as of paramount concern in one section of the United States, the South, where somewhat more than one half the American Negroes still live and where their families were emancipated from slavery slightly less than one hundred years ago.

The disadvantaged status of the Negro community compared with the generality of Americans is thoroughly documented. Equally documented however is the pervasive and rapid improvement in the status of American Negroes. Never have these forces of advancement been so strong as at present, a fact which helps explain the renewed vigor of the counterforces. In a dozen years the instruments of legislation and judicial interpretation have knocked out the so-called "white primary," declared previously segregated public places and transport open to the Negro, and unlocked to him a much wider choice of opportunities for higher education. In addition, the Supreme Court in 1954 invalidated the doctrine of "equal but separate" facilities which had permitted segregated public elementary and high schools. Within a year, over five hundred schools had complied with the Supreme Court decision without fanfare and the process continues steadily. Integration in the armed services, "fair employment practices" legislation in several of the states, and prohibition against job discrimination in any work done by private firms under federal government contract have also markedly raised the status of the Negro. On another front the booming economy, making his labor more in demand, and successive increases in the national minimum wage (now $1 an hour) have brought the Negro to a previously unimagined standard of living.

As a result of all these influences and increasing opportunities, a Negro middle class has over the past two generations been developing. This group is producing a growing number of leaders and participating more fully in the general life of the community. Despite continued restrictions in its access to private housing, this middle class—like the emerging middle classes of the ethnic minorities that had previously entered American society near its bottom rung and gradually climbed up to all its levels—is spreading into better city neighborhoods and into the suburbs of metropolitan centers. It is indisputable that the Negroes, like the Irish, the Italians, the Poles and many others before them, are on their way up.

It is also apparent that the very speed of current advances and the consequent intensity of counterforces will make the Negro problem a turbulent issue for some time to come. With each new skirmish the stereotypes of Negro disabilities may be reinforced. This is particularly significant in Indian-American relations because, in general, Indians' identification of themselves with the Negroes as fellow members of the non-white races is very much stronger than any distinction in Indians' minds between their own status, culture and skills and those of the American Negroes. The converse does not appear to be true. American Negroes, for all their disabilities, tend to think of themselves primarily as Americans and do not identify themselves more with Indians or other colored peoples than with American society generally.

Indians have sometimes also been concerned, as have many Americans, by various discriminations practiced against Asians resident in the United States. While the numbers involved are small—hardly more than a quarter of a million, as compared with fifteen million Negroes—the relatively low traditional economic status of Chinese, Japanese, Filipinos and other Asians in the United States and the legal restrictions on immigration and naturalization have been viewed by Indians as further evidence of "white American" bias. Here again, however, it is true that, while immigration restrictions continue, Asian residents in the United States have increasingly gained equal protection of the law and advanced from modest hereditary occupations to the full range of skills and professions.

Disabilities of disadvantaged groups in Indian society can be dealt with by similar attention to stereotypes and to factual conditions and trends. Through the writings of philosophers, social scientists and journalists, and through missionaries, Americans have known that equal status of all persons was not an ideal of traditional Hindu society, and they have generally deplored that fact. The plethora of caste and class distinctions, the intricacies of exogamous and endogamous social units, the subtle distinctions between sects of the left and those of the right hand, the refusal to take food or water from any but members of certain groups and to permit certain classes of village residents to use the village well—such social stratifications, being alien to all their experience and contrary to their ideals, have repelled many Americans and have induced stereotypes of India as unfavorable as are Indian stereotypes of a "racialist" America.

Americans are also aware of reformist movements, ancient and modern, within Hinduism and of the quickened change that started many decades ago when the impact of the British presence and of Western thought produced a ferment in Indian society that has not yet subsided. Over the decades many beginnings in the direction of reform have been made. In the rapidly filling-up towns caste considerations have become far weaker than they are in the villages. Beginning with Mahatma Gandhi, most Indian leaders have constantly worked to pull down the social barriers which beset the *Harijans*. Independence brought with it a quickened pace of change. The last few years have, for example, seen much legislation and Executive action to combat social disabilities that still survive and to give special protection to the "scheduled castes."

From all this it is possible to conclude that in both countries the combined pressures of humanitarianism, modern social and economic forces and government action are reshaping domestic societies in the direction of more nearly equal status for all citizens. More detailed study would also show that to a remarkable degree—given the

differences in culture and conditions in the two countries
—similar sociological patterns are being traced in this field.
Furthermore, it is impressive to note that the relationship
between social change and coercive legislation does not
appear much different in India from the United States,
even though Indian constitutional principles spell out a
more elaborate range of human rights than does the United
States constitution. In both countries law as an indication
of consensus appears to be more successful in the human
rights field than law as an enforcement of protections in
those cases where they have not yet been fully accepted by
society generally.

It would seem that in the long run neither the disabilities of the American Negro nor the disabilities of some
castes and classes in India need have an adverse effect on
Indian-American relations. Emotional outbursts may continue to occur. But serious students will applaud marks
of progress and deplore setbacks while recognizing that
social change is taking place in both countries in consequence of strong impulses and through somewhat similar
means. It would be well if this process could be made more
widely known among the broad population in both countries.

In the field of human rights measures relating to third
countries, Indian and United States policies most often
intersect in the multilateral meetings of the General Assembly, the Trusteeship Council, and other United Nations organs. The differences between the two countries'
positions turn mainly on three questions: (1) the relation
of such issues as racial discrimination and self-determination to other issues in international affairs; (2) the relation,
undefined in the Charter, between the domestic jurisdiction clause which protects a sovereign state against intervention by United Nations organs and the economic and
social functions given the United Nations which can be
executed only within the territories of sovereign nations;
and (3) the relative effects of international admonition and
of domestic influences on basic social change.

In general, following its domestic emphasis in favor of governmental approaches to social problems, India stands for clear-cut and expanding United Nations jurisdiction over human rights questions, particularly questions of racial discrimination and self-determination, and expects other countries' support as a matter of moral right. In the United States there are more doubts about the capacity of the United Nations to effect basic social changes by the means which India presses. The United States usually takes positions influenced by a more limited reading of the United Nations Charter and seeks to find compromises between the stands taken by the countries normally associated with India and those countries that are their determined opponents. It is not that American and Indian positions are counterposed, but rather that they exhibit variations of emphasis and priority.

India's principal efforts in this field have been devoted to questions of social and political discrimination on racial grounds, particularly of discrimination against persons of Indian origin. The present problems are the result of historic patterns of nineteenth-century emigration from India to other parts of the British Empire, as it then was, that left communities of persons of Indian origin in political jurisdictions with which the present government of India would prefer to deal directly. These include such British colonial areas as Fiji, British Guiana, the West Indies, Zanzibar, Kenya, Uganda, and Tanganyika, as well as India's near neighbors, Burma and Ceylon. Many of these problems do not concern American policy. In the case of South Africa, however, bilateral or Commonwealth negotiations were not successful and India therefore brought the matter before the United Nations in 1946. This action directly involved the United States in the question of the community of Indian origin in the Union of South Africa.

The discrimination against which India has complained is of long duration, reaching back to the mid-nineteenth century. Not long after the ancestors of the present Indian-origin community of some 420,000 persons came to South Africa, at first as contract laborers and then as traders, special restrictions were enacted against them and against their children, although they automatically became South Africans at birth. Persons of Indian origin were debarred from voting, from holding public office, and from apprenticeship or skilled labor posts in factories. They were given only highly restricted rights to hold property, to enter public places and transport, or to obtain a higher education. Recent ghetto measures have further restricted their choice of residence and their business opportunity. Because of its Commonwealth ties, because of Gandhi's experiences in South Africa, because of the principle involved, and because these families originally came from India, the independent Indian government has from the beginning felt a strong, even passionate, interest in the fate of the persons of Indian origin in South Africa and has championed their cause vigorously even though they are not Indian nationals. Thus after some negotiation and after a number of heavier restrictions had been imposed, the Indian government in 1946 withdrew its High Commissioner from South Africa, imposed a trade embargo, and, as has been mentioned earlier, brought the case before the United Nations General Assembly, where it has since remained on the agenda.

The Indian argument in presenting the matter to the United Nations rests on three propositions. First of all, the matter is according to the Indian viewpoint one of proper international concern because equal status for persons of Indian origin assured by the international Capetown Agreements of 1927 and 1932 was violated by unilateral action of the Union of South Africa. Furthermore, even if these agreements did not exist, the Indian stand is that the matter would still be considered of international concern, because of the worsening relations between India and South Africa. Finally, it is the Indian position that the United Nations Charter and the Universal Declaration on Human Rights recognize human rights under international law to such a degree that they can no longer be violated under the rubric of domestic jurisdiction and without incurring the risk of international action and censure. Accordingly, the Indian government made an appeal to the United Nations, under Articles 10 and 14 of the Charter. These major arguments have through the years been advanced by Indian spokesmen with skill, determination and conviction. They are arguments which evoke a fervent response in Indian public opinion.

Americans too are repelled by the excesses and repressions practiced by the South African government. However the United States has taken a relatively mild position that also rests on three major considerations. First of all is the American view that conditions of international and domestic politics generally call for support of a fairly broad interpretation of the domestic jurisdiction clause of the Charter. Secondly, there is the doubt felt in the United States whether the United Nations can through the means available to it accomplish the kind of positive results in the field of human rights that the Indian government desires; the converse is the fear that criticism without implementation may have the dangerous effect of encouraging extremist groups and of solidifying opinion in resistance against "outside" criticism. The third consideration is closely related to the second and rests on the conviction that no nation at present can or will exert enough pressure on South Africa by any means to force a fundamental change in its social organization; and that indeed internal developments appear to be the most likely instrument of any change that may occur. However, these arguments do not produce any satisfaction in India because Indians feel that Americans have not attached enough weight to their complaint of a unilateral modification of an international agreement.

While the issue of South African treatment of persons of Indian origin has caused irritation between India and the United States, particularly on the public opinion level and particularly in India, it is worth noting that with the passage of years since India first moved the matter in the United Nations the actual policies pursued by the two countries have gradually become more similar. For example, without conceding its major principles, India has, perhaps because of its increasing preoccupation with other international issues, moderated its direct complaints against South Africa. While there is no reason to believe that India may not continue to urge the United States to take a firmer line against South Africa's actions, it is also not likely that the South African question will again cause major disturbances in Indian-American relations.

In another area of human rights the relative positions of India and the United States are sharply different and the differences attract sharp comment in both countries. This is in respect to the attitude of the Soviet-bloc countries toward human rights. Examples that have come before the United Nations include: violations of human rights in Eastern Europe, the ILO-ECOSOC report on the existence of forced labor in the Soviet Union, the question of atrocities committed against prisoners of war in the Korean conflict, and the question of restrictions placed on the liberty of Soviet wives of foreign nationals to leave the Soviet Union with their husbands.

It has been the American position that forced labor bears so close a resemblance to slavery, which for generations has been regarded as a fit subject of international action, that it has a rightful place on the agenda of the United Nations. It was also the American position that the Korean war prisoners issue deserved international airing. More generally, it is the American position that violations of human rights by the Soviet powers call for world consideration as symptomatic of new oppressions, in contrast to the steady withering away of traditional colonialism.

It has been the Indian position that these cases were only ammunition in the cold war. In their consideration, the Indian delegates have remained silent, abstained, or, in the case of the forced labor report, disavowed the Indian chairman of the investigating committee and denounced the "misleading" and "deliberately set up selectivity" of the area of inquiry into the subject. The United States did not agree that the charges against Soviet violations of human rights should be left without examination.

Differences of focus between Indian and American approaches to human rights have come out perhaps most clearly in recent years in the lengthy United Nations consideration of a universal covenant on human rights. The main principles under debate have been the role of an international organization in furthering human welfare and the ranking of priorities among the various human rights being considered. We can profitably refer to some of the items involved before returning to these principles.

Throughout the discussions of an international bill of human rights, India's vigorous lead has been in the direction of a broad interpretation of the desirable scope of United Nations action. Indian delegates have appealed for United Nations action on behalf of freedom, the dignity of individuals, and a host of other generalized rights. In short, they have sought—along with other Asian nations as well as Middle Eastern and Latin American nations—to create treaties which like their own constitution would contain a broad statement of the goals to be achieved; they have sought to erect a standard in the human rights field toward which all peoples could strive.

Acting on this pattern, Indian delegates succeeded in incorporating into the draft human rights covenants such goals as the "right of peoples and nations to self-determination as a prerequisite to the full enjoyment of all fundamental human rights." To implement this principle, India has favored an international human rights body to which individual complaints could be carried without clearance with national governments. Furthermore, the Indian government has pressed tirelessly for increased United Nations supervision over the processes by which any people could be helped toward self-determination.

It has also been the Indian position, taken in discussion on the draft convention on political rights of women, that

the rights expressed for women generally should be stipu-
lated to be extended to women in non-self-governing and
trust territories. On freedom of information, however,
it has been the Indian position that governments should
be given a right of international correction of distortions
in news reporting. This has been regarded as a problem
particularly for the underdeveloped countries, and the
suggested remedy as a further step toward equal status.

The United States position on these issues has been
rather more limited and reserved. Rather than pressing
for a "maximum" definition of world-wide human rights
through United Nations action, the United States has followed the patterns of its constitutional structure and taken
a stand for treaty provisions that would provide a "floor"
to support the relatively few civil and political rights
that are generally—at least in nontotalitarian societies—accepted throughout the world. Similarly, and in contrast to
India and other Asian states, the United States has stood
for a cautious attitude toward the implementation of such
a treaty, refusing to go beyond a narrowly defined complaint procedure. Thus the United States has resisted
broad interpretations of women's rights conventions, the
power of governments to "correct" international news
communications, and the authority of the United Nations
to force the pace of self-determination in dependent areas.

Similarly, when debate developed over the relative priority of self-determination and other human rights, considerable differences of principle between Indian and
American positions became apparent. It is the Indian position that self-determination is the necessary basis for all
other human rights, and that it therefore must be the primary objective of all efforts to expand human rights. On
this position India stands firm with the prevailing views
of the Asian and African states that were represented at
the Bandung Conference. The American position, while
agreeing to the principle of self-determination, is somewhat different—a position that lies between the views sub-
scribed to by India and those of some of the United States'

allies in Europe. It is that all human rights are closely related, that adequate institutions of justice, community
willingness to finance their own affairs, and protection for
minorities are inescapable components of viable self-determination.

In principle, the Indian rejection of this American position rests on the assumption that the American stand supports and shelters delaying tactics by administering powers
whose vested interests oppose dependent peoples' will to
self-determination. In principle, India has in the past
favored direct United Nations guardianship for all dependent peoples—without the interposition of administering powers. India also favors supervision of all dependent
peoples by the Trusteeship Council, although this is considered less satisfactory because of the influence therein of
the major colonial powers. As a minimum, India would
support a steady expansion of international supervision
and control of dependent areas through the procedural
provisions relating to trust and non-self-governing territories. Here again, in principle, the United States has resisted the enlargement of United Nations governmental
functions in this field, on the familiar ground that the
United Nations is not an agency for superseding existing
sovereignties.

In practice, India and the United States have worked
more closely together on problems relating to the trust and
non-self-governing territories than their differences of
viewpoint would seem to indicate. Possible patterns for
the future can be observed in India's support of American
efforts in the Trusteeship Council to moderate disputes
and to find ways of assisting the movement of areas toward
self-government but with preparatory periods and without
trying to commit the administering powers to the obligation of carrying out the principles advocated by India.

So much for the high points of the record to date. What
are the implications for Indian-American relations? In
their approaches to domestic human rights policies, the
differences between the domestic constitutional systems

of India and the United States are greater than between their methods of implementing social advances. Similarly, in the international human rights field, the evidence suggests that Indian-American differences are greatest on such broad topics as the jurisdiction and powers of the United Nations and least where concrete economic, social and international pressures are involved. When the issue is one of interpreting the Charter's domestic jurisdiction clause and defining the economic and social functions of the United Nations, India can be expected to stand for their expansion, while the United States can be expected to take a stand in favor of a more limited construction. But where the issue involved is, say, discrimination in South Africa, broad agreement between India and the United States can be assumed on the propositions that the *apartheid* system is unjust, that because of modern social and economic pressures, as well as humanitarian impulses and other forces, it is self-defeating and cannot endure, and that to the extent that foreign and international action can make an effective, constructive contribution, such action should be encouraged. Both the United States and India have laid more emphasis on these points in recent years than they did in the first years in which the South African case was raised before the United Nations.

The importance of human rights as a field of interaction between Indian and American principles, policies and interests cannot be overemphasized. In spite of some differences, the two countries share the common goal of a steady expansion of human rights both at home and throughout the world. Despite divergences in what each would call the "moral eyesight" of the other, and in their approaches to the role of the United Nations and to the range of international action in human rights issues, India and the United States can, on the basis of their past records, be assumed to work more closely in practice on these problems than they may stand in their general approach to dealing with them.

Chapter 9

CONCLUSION

THE PRECEDING chapters have shown the common ground and the differences that have characterized Indian-American relations. They have traced the development of the considerations that persuaded the United States to abandon its traditional policies and assume in peacetime the heavy burden of military preparedness and of unparalleled foreign economic assistance. They have also traced the reasons that have since 1947 prompted India to put its faith in the *Pancha Shil* and to decide that it would try to serve as a "bridge" between the two sides in the cold war.

This past pattern has revealed a number of differences, both as to understanding and as to foreign policy. In matters of understanding and interpretation it has been the issues of communism and of broad security policies that have in the past caused the most concern. As for the first, in spite of abiding differences concerning the intentions of Communist powers, India and the United States have since 1956 been drawn a degree closer by the force of events. Since the denunciation of Stalin at the Twentieth Communist Party Congress in February of that year, more and more Indians have come to question Communist claims. The intervention of Soviet troops in the Hungarian national rising produced further disenchantment. Thus, although wide differences remain, at least in some ways India and the United States have come somewhat closer together in their evaluation of the Soviet Union.

In the matter of broad security policies, however, no

such degree of *rapprochement* has taken place. While not arguing in the least about policies of protection against attack from immediate neighbors, the two nations were and continue to be very far apart in their attitudes toward nuclear weapons and toward security policies in the former colonial areas of Asia and Africa. India stands for immediate nuclear disarmament and the prohibition of the testing of nuclear weapons. The Indian government also believes that, since war can no longer "solve" broad international disputes without mutual destruction, the method of conciliation must take its place. The United States on the other hand, while abhorring war and striving for disarmament, feels that peace can best be preserved through deterrent power which would curb a would-be aggressor. It is safe to predict that Americans would welcome any disarmament or nuclear control plan that effectively safeguards this capability but would reject all proposals whose effect would be to diminish its relative capacity to deter aggression.

In point of fact, it seems to many Americans that there is exact agreement between the *principle* of American strategy toward the Soviet Union and the principle of Indian strategy toward Pakistan. The differences come in implementation. And here we encounter not only nuclear weaponry as contrasted to "conventional" weaponry, but also the fact that the Indian security problem, so far as it relates to Pakistan, can be met within the territory of India and the surrounding seas whereas the American security problem must, by its nature and because of the reliance of many non-Communist countries on the American deterrent power, spread across several continents.

Security agreements involving countries in Asia as well as other continents might not seem so urgent to Americans if the "atomic stalemate" made all other military strategy irrelevant. In fact, the postwar Soviet record suggests to many Americans that this "stalemate" might well lead the Russians to conclude that they could safely undertake a limited aggression—say in Iran—on the assumption that the United States would not expose Detroit to atomic retaliation and destruction in order to save Isfahan. Therefore these Americans believe that the free world must also have the means of meeting lesser aggression by measures short of all-out war. Hence the stationing of American troops abroad, the creation of indigenous forces, and, to some extent, the building of bases.

To many Indians this argument is shaky. They doubt the premises and feel that harmful side-effects of the policy have been ignored. Thus, many Indians question whether Soviet aggressiveness can or should be assumed as a fact of international politics; they are persuaded that Russia has no aggressive intentions against India and its immediate neighbors. Furthermore, as we have seen, Indians tend to feel that pacts between the powerful United States and small, weak countries, especially in Asia, are likely to result in the subordination of the Asian countries' interests to those of the United States. By emphasizing military preparedness, these pacts—in the Indian view—divert needed resources from economic development. Furthermore, as the military capacity of such nations grows with American help, they become stronger not only against the threat of Soviet expansion but also in relation to their immediate neighbors—and the consequences of such changing power balances may disrupt regional relationships. These political complications, of which Indians became most sharply aware through the American military assistance program in Pakistan, fortify an already-strong Indian view that the fresh establishment of American arms in Asia, coming immediately after white armies have been forced out of Asia by the sweep of nationalism, is repugnant. If America, as it professes, wants to help Asia, it should, in this view, concentrate on providing badly-needed economic and technical assistance.

But, ask the Americans, is it really correct to treat military measures on the one hand and economic development and peaceful settlement of disputes on the other as alternative approaches to basic world problems? To be sure, just what should be done in any particular area or country in the balancing of military and economic measures is always debatable. Whether or not foreign assistance is available, there is the continuing problem of limited resources and competing demands, and often there is room for differences in emphasis. But most Americans are convinced that underlying all the specific cases is a world situation in which the success of any one of these lines of actions is dependent on the concurrent pursuit of the other. Military defense alone will not suffice to build democracy and true security in the free world. But neither will measures of economic development alone provide basic security. The two must be considered together. Most Indians, however, hold—pointing to their own experience— that concurrent pursuit of military measures and economic development is impossible in the case of small new countries of Asia, while limited measures of defense against local rivals may be attempted.

It comes down to this: Americans and Indians agree that negotiation and persuasion are possible means of settling some issues with the Communist powers, but most Indians argue that the United States should lay more emphasis on these means, at least where Asia is involved, whereas it is believed in the United States that free-world countries can hope for a satisfactory solution on major issues only when they are in a position to prevent the Soviet Union from getting any major part of the result it wants by use of force—or at least to make the process so costly as to dissuade the Soviet Union from undertaking aggression.

In addition to these questions of interpretation and understanding, the two nations have been sharply divided on policy matters concerning the Soviet Union and China on the one hand and Pakistan on the other. In part these differences arise from the differences in interpretation mentioned above, in part they arise from differing estimates of the national security and its requirements. Since these policy differences are the expressions of strongly held and widely supported convictions among the two peoples

—convictions to which they have been brought by their particular experiences—it is unlikely that either will discount at the other's bidding the threat which it sees in these countries or that it will lower its guard. Only distinct and dependable improvements in the two situations, which reassure the United States and India respectively, are likely to produce any significant policy changes and, consequently, to bring the two nations closer on these matters.

These differences have not however prevented India and the United States from cooperating on some major issues. In the Suez crisis of 1956 the two nations worked along similar lines. American policy in this instance startled Indian opinion and won more respect for the United States in India than any other American action in recent years. The Nehru-Eisenhower conference in December of the same year was a welcome indication of the interest the two leaders felt in closer contact and more intimate exchange of views. Although it is obviously impossible to be categorical about the results of the talks, it is a matter of record that since that conference the two governments have shown noticeable restraint in their official comments on each other's policies. As examples, one might adduce Indian comments on the so-called Eisenhower Doctrine and on developments in the Middle East, and American comments during and just after the Security Council debates on Kashmir in early 1957. For whatever reason, there is little doubt that for the time being at least there is a greater willingness on the part of the United States and India to live with their policy differences—and this is a welcome development.

In speaking of cooperation between the two nations it is also important to point out that the differences that have existed between India and the United States have not prevented the flow of substantial American economic aid to India. Indeed, an increasing number of Americans are watching with keen interest India's efforts at economic development, believing that India's success could serve as a demonstration to other underdeveloped areas of the possibilities inherent in a democratic political process. It is of course recognized on both sides that there are problems and difficulties ahead and there are some differences as to how best to deal with them.

It is clear that in the future the interest of India and the United States will be locked together even more closely by the compulsions of geography, communications and world politics. The two nations may need each other's cooperation in some crucial ways—in matters of peace and war and in dealing with problems that will be encountered by the newly independent states. Furthermore, there is no reason to doubt that India and the United States will continue to be strongly attracted to each other by the similarity in their ideals, their mutual abhorrence of war and aggression, and their common concern that Asia as well as other parts of the world should grow in economic health and political stability.

In discussing differences and similarities between the two countries it is of course insufficient to stop with policy matters. Equally and sometimes more important in determining differences and in improving relations are the concepts of each other held by the peoples of the nations involved. Here we are dealing with intangibles, but since India and the United States are in truth just coming to know each other, the field needs exploration. It is not too much to hope that an improvement in communication between the two peoples can and will lead to a better and more sympathetic understanding of the problems and anxieties that beset each of them.

In earlier chapters there has been reference—perhaps too much reference—to "the" Indian view and "the" American view of various issues. This is of course too sharp a dichotomy. The millions of people in either country have their individual opinions and emotions, which are often imprecise and ambivalent. Even the thousands in each country who have come into personal contact with the other tend to make their appraisals on the basis of mental images, stereotypes, and individual contacts that both attract and repel them.

If you were to ask one hundred Indians how they imagine the United States, the responses would vary greatly. Many would know the names of Washington, Franklin and Lincoln as well as of more recent Americans. The American Declaration of Independence and Bill of Rights would doubtless have impressed some of them. Many would describe the United States as a vigorous country which has grown rapidly to a position of great power, and they might admire or fear this growth, or both. Some would argue that the United States in recent years has become imperialist, an international meddler, a warmonger. (A limited public opinion poll taken in West Bengal in 1955 shocked Americans with its report that a high percentage of those questioned regarded American policies as the most likely cause for a third world war.) Many others, however, while suggesting that the United States does sometimes "throw its weight about" and is not above using economic assistance for political leverage, would quickly deny that the more extreme beliefs represent Indian thinking generally. Quite a few would hold that the policies of the United States, more than of any other nation, can determine whether the world will have peace or war and prosperity or poverty. They would probably admit to fearing as well as appreciating such great power. Still others would base their comments on the images of American gangsters of the prohibition era—an image that has been made familiar through American films.

If, reversing the process, you were to ask one hundred Americans how they imagine India, the replies would be equally diverse. Although India has not until recent years impinged so strongly on the consciousness of most Americans as, say, China, quite a few would refer to varying early impressions gained from Kipling or missionaries on furlough. The names of Gandhi and, after him, Nehru would be widely known. There would be a widespread impression of India's poverty but a good many would also mention India's recent independence and its experiment in democracy, its strong push for economic development, and its efforts to modernize its social system as well. Some would talk of India's foreign policy, and among these a number would doubtless describe it as being "soft" on communism. While some would talk of India's "annexation" of Kashmir, others would show more concern with India's being "neutral—leaning the other way." At the same time there would probably be more appreciation than a few years ago of the reasons for India's policy of nonalignment.

Beneath such impressions as these undoubtedly lie others that may have even stronger effect on the attitudes held in one country toward the other. It would be misleading, for example, to discount the distrust of power or the strong sensitivity to domination of colored peoples by white peoples that are deeply imbedded in Indian culture. Similarly, it would be deceptive to ignore the continuing influence on American policy of the cultural and emotional ties that exist between the bulk of the American people and the peoples of Europe.

Certainly, the understanding of each other's aspirations, emotions and outlooks which in the long run must underlie sound relations has yet far to go in both nations. Lasting change in these difficult matters can be expected to come only slowly. Even so, there are steps that India and the United States are taking and can take to speed the process.

Contacts between the people of the two countries are growing apace. Since World War II a good many Indian students—currently about 2,500 a year—have gone to the United States for education and training. Citizens of India by the hundreds have seen the United States through diplomatic missions to Washington or to the United Nations or through business, scientific, technological or academic assignments. Similarly, many more Americans than before have recently come to know India at first hand, either through consultative missions, as students, or—in increasing numbers—as tourists. Indian art and textile exhibitions in the United States and the appearance of a leading Indian dancer on Broadway are balanced by visits of an American ballet group or symphony orchestra to Indian cities.

It is true that some Indians in America and some Americans in India have difficult, even distasteful, experiences. Yet the weight of evidence is all on the side of satisfaction and profit in these personal exchanges. They seem to be generally most successful when the visitors and their hosts are engaged in common tasks. For an Indian student in the United States there should probably be less concern about the ideological meeting of minds and more about the activities that he engages in, such as, for example, the study of engineering.

More can be done in both countries in education. In American schools little has been taught about the history of India, its traditions, and its form of government. Nor have United States history and institutions figured much in Indian curricula, which have been traditionally dominated by a British approach.

Even in the day-to-day flow of news between the two countries much remains to be achieved. The cost of maintaining overseas correspondents is admittedly high, but direct interpretation of the American scene by more than one or two Indian correspondents and wider coverage of India for Americans—not just to explain political issues or to note sensational events, but to give some sense of the variety of human experience—should be within the available resources.

In spite of recent efforts to promote public knowledge and appreciation of the cultural achievements and living conditions of the two peoples, little more than a beginning has been made. Although some things can be done by governments, much more can be expected from private effort along various lines: in the universities, in business and professional contacts, in the field of public entertainment, and through firsthand experience of actual conditions in India and the United States. Through this expansion of personal experience in many fields, mutual respect and appreciation can develop and unreal stereotypes be moderated if not removed. And this expansion of contacts can be important also in policy terms because they can provide a sound basis for the realistic consideration of differences in policy and the reasons for these differences. This is not to suggest that good cultural relations will eliminate differences in policy.

Despite the differences of approach and of policy that have so far troubled Indian-American relations and that may for some time continue to do so, this study has shown that the mutual interests of India and the United States far outweigh the differences, that it is strongly in the interests of both India and the United States for the two countries to cooperate effectively on important world problems, and that the mutual advantage of cooperation is being increasingly recognized in both countries as their policy interests touch at a growing number of points. There is clear evidence that both peoples wish profoundly to live in a world of peace and progress. Despite difficulties they should be able to work toward this goal in closer cooperation in the future than they have in the past.

INDEX

Accession of princely states, general, Lord Mountbatten on, 76; *see also* individual states
Acheson, Dean, on NATO (1950), 52; on "defense perimeter" (1950), 118
Aggression, limited, 185
Agricultural Commodities Agreement (1956), 153
Aid, economic, *see* Colombo Plan, economic aid, economic development, International Bank, Point Four, private investment, SUNFED, UN Expanded Technical Assistance Program
Algeria, 165-167
ANZUS Pact, 134
Asian-Arab group, 161; *see also* Bandung Conference
Asian Relations Conference (1947), 99
Atomic energy, 46
Atomic stalemate, 62, 185

Baghdad Pact, 56, 62; and Pakistan, 91
Bandung Conference (1955), and China, 131
Bao Dai, 127
Belgian Congo, 163
Berlin Blockade (1948–1949), 34, 50-51
Bhutan, Indian treaty with (1949), 114
Bill of Rights, U.S., 170
Bose, Subhas Chandra, 22
Brussels Pact (1948), 50
Bulganin, N. A., 22, 64
Burma, 95, 158; Communist threat to, 131; debt to India (1937), 132; loan from India, 132
Byrnes, James F., policy of "patience and firmness" (1946), 46

Cairo Conference (1943), on Formosa, 108
Cambodia, 95, 127
Capitalism, suspicion of, 141-142; *see also* private enterprise
Central Intelligence Agency, 28
Ceylon, 95, 158
Chiang Kai-Shek, 97, 98, 108
China, Nationalist, *see* Formosa
China, People's Republic of, 34, 95-96, 101-102; as India's rival, 102-103; system of government, 102; economic development, 103; applicability of methods to India, 103; Indian policy toward, 135; U.S. policy toward, 136
"China Question," 96-97
Churchill, Winston, 108; speech at Fulton (1946), 43-44
Civil liberties, British influence, 5; state and, 5; economic organization and, 6
Coexistence, emphasis on by Soviet leaders, 64; Indian and American interpretation, 64-65; *see also* Hungarian uprising (1956)
Colombo Plan, 132, 148
Colonialism, 96; Soviet Union and, 38-39; in Indochina, Indian attitude on, 126; general Indian stand, 156; American tradition, 156; "new colonialism," 156, 157; general American policy, 157; general Indian and American objectives, 162, 166; prospects, 167-168,

185; post-colonial problems, 168; *see also* human rights, Indochina, United Nations

Cominform, 49

Commonwealth of Nations, 177

Communal outbreaks (1947), 80

Communism, evaluation of as threat, 9; "mellowing" of, 62-63; liberalization, 64-65; and economic aid, 140, 141; *see also* Communist Party of India; China, People's Republic of; Hungarian uprising (1956)

Communism, domestic, hostility to in India, 36-37; in the U.S., 37-38

Communism, international, interpretation in India, 38-39, 40; in U.S., 39-40

Communism and Asia, Indian criticism of U.S. policies, 55-56; U.S. policies, 56-57; world-wide war and, 57

Communist Party of India, 22; wartime collaboration with British, 37; Preventive Detention Act, and, 37; and Kerala State (1957), 37

Companies Act of 1956, 147

Congress (U.S.), and Executive, 28-29; Senate and foreign policy, 29-30; House of Representatives and foreign policy, 30; committees, investigations by, 30-31; *see also* elective system

Congress party, 3; and formation of foreign policy, 15-16; and Kashmir accession, 76

Containment, policy of, 47

Cultural exchange, 190-192

Cyprus, 164

Diem, Ngo Dinh, *see* Ngo

Directive Principles, Indian constitution, 171

Dixon, Sir Owen, 81; on Kashmir dispute, 78, 82

Domestic jurisdiction, *see* United Nations

Dulles, John Foster, 32; and Soviet intentions, 42; and Communist threat to Southeast Asia (1954), 129

Economic aid by U.S., role in Indian development, 138; Indian fears of, 138; U.S. policies on, 139-141; military and economic, 140; Indian criticisms, 140-141; U.S. government, 148-149; amount of aid to Asia, 150-151; granting methods, criticism of, 151; Soviet aid, 151-152; to Southeast Asia, 132; and economic development, 138; *see also* private investment, Point Four, etc.

Economic development, and foreign aid, 138; U.S. concern over, 139-141

Economic organization, 6

Economic strength, effect on foreign policy, 7-9; Indian relations with China, 136

Education, "equal but separate" doctrine, 172

Education, recommendation on, 191-192

Egypt, U.S. reaction to invasion (1956), 167

Eisenhower, Dwight D., 32; and Suez Canal crisis, 67; on arms aid to Pakistan, 87-88; conference with Nehru (1956), 188

Elective system (legislators), in India, 27; in the United States, 31-32

Fair Employment Practices (U.S.), 172

Five Year Plans (India), effects of on Asia and Africa, 13; problems facing, 145

Forced labor, ILO-ECOSOC Report on, 179-180

Foreign policy, formation of, in India, 26-27; in United States, 27; opposition, 22; open debate and, 32-33; *see also* Congress (U.S.), House of the People, public opinion, separation of powers

Formosa, historical background, 107-108; Nationalist position, 108; Communist position, 108-109; In-

dian attitude, 109; *see also* United States and China
French West Africa, 163

Gandhi, Mahatma, 41, 58, 80, 174, 177
Geneva Agreements (1954), U.S. attitude toward, 128, 129; Indian attitude toward, 128-129; Diem and, 130; Ho Chi Minh and, 130; *see also* International Commissions for Supervision and Control of Viet Nam, Laos and Cambodia
Goa, 164; Dulles statement on (1955), 164
Graham, Dr. Frank, 81

Harijans, 174
Ho Chi Minh, 127; India and, 128-129
House of the People, 26-27; discussion in, 27; party discipline in, 27; organization of, 26-27; relation to Executive, 27-28
Human rights, Indian and American concepts, 169-171; racial discrimination in U.S., 171-173; caste system, 174-175
Human rights in UN, and domestic jurisdiction, 175; as international concern, 175; Indian position, 176; U.S. position, 176; persons of Indian origin in the Union of South Africa, 176-179; Covenant, 180, 181; political rights of women, 180-181; freedom of information, 181; trusteeships and, 182; Indian and American concepts, 183
Hungarian uprising (1956), 34, 185; and "liberalization," 40; effect in India, 65-66, 71; and the United States, 66-67
Hyderabad, 37, 41, 69; and Kashmir dispute, 75

India and "Bridge" policy, 58-59, 60, 184; criticisms of, 59; support for, 59-60; blocs and mediation, 60
India and "cold war," aloofness, 41; evaluation of, 54-55

India and Communist China, reaction to Communist victory, 99-101, 102; recognition (1949), 100; China as Indian rival, 101; *see also* United States and China; China, People's Republic of; *Pancha Shil*
India and Republic of China, historical background to 1949, 97-98, 99
India and Russia, 186; lack of contact, 53; admiration for, 53
Indian origin, communities of, in British colonies, 176; in Burma, 176; in Ceylon, 176; in South Africa, 176-179; UN case: Indian position, 177-178; U.S. position, 178-179
Indochina, 158; U.S. help, 127; Chinese Communist help, 127; Geneva Conference (1954), 128; Indian role at Geneva Conference, 128; Geneva Agreements, 128-129; future of, 129; *see also* Viet Nam, Laos, Cambodia, International Commissions
Indonesia, 95, 158; Communist activities in, 131; and Overseas Chinese, 131; independence struggle, 158-160
Industrial Credit and Investment Corporation of India (1955), 144
Internal Security Act of 1950, 37
International Bank for Reconstruction and Development, 144, 149
International Commissions for Supervision and Control of Viet Nam, Laos and Cambodia, Indian role in, 130; activities of, 130-131
International Finance Corporation of India (1948), 144, 149
Italian colonies, 158; in United Nations, 161-162
Italian Somaliland, 161

Jana Sangh, 22
Japan, 95, 96
Jarring, Gunnar, and Kashmir dispute, 81-82, 85; and U.S. arms aid to Pakistan, 87
Junagadh, 69; and Kashmir dispute, 75, 76

Kashmir, 69, 70; U.S. attitude, 70; integration with India, 79, 83, 85-86; importance to India, 79-80
Kashmir dispute, before Security Council, 71-74, 81; accession to India, 72-73, 75, 76; plebiscite in, 73, 74, 75, 77-78, 81, 82-83, 85; UNCIP, 74; Indian criticism of U.S. position, 74-78; UNCIP Resolution (August 13, 1948), 77, 81, 82; UNCIP Resolution (January 5, 1949), 77, 81, 82; and communal tension, 78-79, 86; American attitudes on, 79-85; mediation efforts, 81; plebiscite in Vale, 86; and U.S. arms aid to Pakistan, 88; see also accession of princely states, Hyderabad, Junagadh
Khrushchev, Nikita, 22, 40; Indian trip (1955–1956), 64
Korea, 95, 96-100; North Korean attack, reactions to, 117, 118, 125; UN Commission, 117; U.S. and United Korea, 117; UN and unification, 118; U.S. help to, 118, 119-120; India and use of force, 120-121; 38th Parallel, 121; Chinese "volunteers," 122; efforts to halt fighting, 122-123; Chinese aggression, Indian interpretation of, 123; "Great Debate," 123-124; armistice negotiations, 124; repatriation of prisoners of war, 124-125; Neutral Nations Repatriation Commission, 125
Korean prisoners of war, 179

Laos, 95, 127
Lenin, on war and imperialism, 38
Libya, 161

Malaya, 95, 158, 162; Communist threat to, 131
Marshall, George C., 49-50
Marshall Plan, 33, 47-48, 50; and Eastern Europe, 49; reaction of French and Italian Communist parties, 49; see also Molotov, V. M.
Masaryk, Jan, 49
McNaughton, General A. G. L., 81

Menon, V. K. Krishna, 23
Molotov, V. M., 48-49
Monroe Doctrine, 156
Morocco and Tunisia, 158; in United Nations, 160-161
Moslem League, and Kashmir accession, 76
Mountbatten, Lord Louis, on accession of princely states, 76

National Industrial Development Corporation (1954), 144
National Security Council (U.S.), 28
National Small Industries Corporation (1955), 144
NATO, 33, 51-52, 56; as "colonial" alliance, 53, 61; and Goa, 164
Nehru, Jawaharlal, 2; and shaping of foreign policy attitudes, 20-21; and successor, 23; and Soviet Union, 39; on democracy in India, 39; and U.S. arms aid to Pakistan, 87, 88, 89, 90; and Communist China, 97, 98, 103; on Tibet and Nepal (1950), 113; on Communism and colonialism, 157; on Indonesian independence struggle, 158
Nepal, 95; Nehru statement (1950), 113; Indian treaty with (1950), 114; Indian policy toward, 115; Indian goals in, 115
Ngo Dinh Diem, 109, 127; India and, 128, 130; U.S. and, 129, 130
Nixon, Richard M., 32
Nonalignment, 3, 9; and American isolationism, 3-4; Pakistan and, 91; U.S. economic aid and, 139, 141
North Atlantic Treaty Organization, see NATO
Northeast Frontier Area, Tibet, 111-113, 116; domestic protective measures, 113-114; Bhutan, 114; Sikkim, 114; Nepal, 114-115; general considerations, 115-116

Pacts, military, 35, 61; fear of, 60; U.S. system in Asia, 62; Indian objections to, 62-63; see also Pakistan and U.S.
Pakistan, 9, 35; pact with U.S., 89;

U.S. attitude on pact, 90; Indian reaction, 90

Pakistan and India, disputes, summarized, 69; relative strength, 90, 91; military and economic aid, relation of, 92-93

Pakistan and United States, U.S. arms aid to, 86, 87-88; pact with U.S., 89; U.S. attitude on pact, 90; Indian reaction, 90-92; military and economic aid, relation of, 92-93

Pancha Shil (Five Principles), 58, 101, 132, 184; agreements, 132; concept of, 132-133; U.S. reactions to, 133

Partition (1947), 69

Persons of Indian origin in the Union of South Africa, see Indian origin

Philippine Republic, 95, 96, 109, 158; Communist threat to, 131

Point Four, 33

Portuguese East and West Africa, 163

Potsdam Conference (1945), 43; on Formosa, 108

Press, and influence on foreign policy in India, 23

Preventive Detention Act, 37

Private enterprise, American attitude, 142; Indian reaction, 142-143, 144; see also capitalism

Private investment, 6; conditions for, 145; Indian attitudes, 146; American investment in India, 146-147; future, 153

Private organizations, 145

Public opinion and foreign policy, in India, 14-15, 16-18; in the United States, 18-19, 25-26; private organizations and, 24-25; West Bengal poll (1955), 190

Puerto Rico, 156

Razakars, 41

Reparations, 46

Revolution, American, 3-4, 156

Rhee, Syngman, 109, 118

Rio Treaty (1947), 50

Roosevelt, Franklin D., 2, 108; on Yalta Conference, 43

Satyagraha, 58

SEATO, 56, 62, 134; and Pakistan, 91; Dulles on Communist threat (1954), 129; Indian reaction to, 134

Second Statement of Governmental Industrial Policy (1956), 147

Security, 8-9; social and economic threats to, 12; and Pakistan, 70-71; and Tibet, 113; and Bhutan and Sikkim, 114; and Nepal, 115; buffer states and, 116; Indian-Chinese relations, 135-136; and Tibet, 136; conclusions, 184, 185

Self-determination, and Woodrow Wilson, 156; and covenant on human rights, 180; priority of, 181-182; trusteeship and, 182

Separation of powers, 28-30

Sikkim, Indian Treaty with (1950), 114

Singapore, 95

Sino-Soviet relations, Sino-Soviet alliance, 100; effect of recognition on, 106

Socialistic pattern of society, 6, 142; and Communist economic theory, 39-40

Socialists, 22

Southeast Asia, Indian policies in, 126, 131; U.S. policies in, 126, 131-132, 134; Communist threat, 129, 131

Southeast Asia Collective Defense Treaty, see SEATO

Southwest Africa, 164-165

Soviet expansion (1945–1949), Eastern Europe, 43; Azerbaijan, 43; Greece, 43, 46; pressure on Turkey, 43; in Manchuria, 43; in Korea, 43; effect on U.S. public opinion, 45; and peace treaties, 46; Eastern Europe, treaties with, 49; Czechoslovakia, 49; see also Berlin Blockade, India and Russia

Soviet-American relations (1945–1949), U.S. assumptions (1945), 42

Soviet wives of foreign nationals, 179-180
Stalin, Joseph, 43
State economic activities, in India, 143-144; uncertainties over, in U.S., 144
SUNFED (Special United Nations Fund for Economic Development), 149
Suez Canal crisis (1956), 34; and India, 65; and United States, 66-67; conclusions, 188

Tagore, Rabindranath, 98
Tandon, Purshottam Das, 22
Teheran Conference (1943), 43
Thailand, 95, 96; and "Free Thai" government, 131
Tibet, 96, 108, 136; background to 1950, 111; Communist takeover, 112; Indian reaction, 112-113; effect on Indian-U.S. relations, 116
Trade, Indian-American, 137-138, 153
Truman Doctrine, 33; and Greece and Turkey, 46-47
Truman, Harry S., 43; warning to Congress (1945), 45-46, 48
Trusteeship system, 163; Indian and U.S. attitudes, 163
Twentieth Communist Party Congress (1956), 40; and coexistence, 64; conclusions, 184
Two-nation theory, and Kashmir dispute, 76, 79

United Nations, 9-11; great power unanimity in, 10-11; as enforcement agency, 11; Morocco and Tunisia, 160-161; Italian colonies, 161-162; Algeria, 165-167; domestic jurisdiction, 166, 178; see also trusteeship system
UN Economic Commission for Asia and the Far East, 134
UN Expanded Technical Assistance Program, 149
UNRRA, 47, 48, 149
United States, and alliances, 51-52; and negotiation, 52
United States and China, background to 1949, 98-99; reaction to Communist victory, 99, 100, 102; Mutual Defense Pact (1954), 109-110; see also Formosa; China, People's Republic of; Pancha Shil
United States and isolation, retreat from, 44
Universal Declaration on Human Rights, 177; and UN Charter, 177
Untouchability, 171

Vandenberg, Senator Arthur H., on Soviet expansion, 47
Viet Nam, 95, 127; North Viet Nam, 96; South Viet Nam, and Geneva Agreements, 128; and elections, 129; and supervision of, 130-131; U.S. economic aid, 132; see also Indochina

Welfare, goals of Indian constitution, 143; see also state economic activities
West Asia and India, 91
Western New Guinea, 165

Yalta Conference (1945), 43

Zhdanov, Andrei, 19